BUILDING TRUE COMMUNITY

Thirty Years Down the Road Less Traveled

EVE BERRY

ARCHWAY
PUBLISHING

This book is a work of non-fiction. Unless otherwise noted, the author and the publisher make no explicit guarantees as to the accuracy of the information contained in this book and in some cases, names of people and places have been altered to protect their privacy.

Archway Publishing books may be ordered through booksellers or by contacting:

Archway Publishing
1663 Liberty Drive
Bloomington, IN 47403
www.archwaypublishing.com
844-669-3957

Because of the dynamic nature of the Internet, any web addresses or links contained in this book may have changed since publication and may no longer be valid. The views expressed in this work are solely those of the author and do not necessarily reflect the views of the publisher, and the publisher hereby disclaims any responsibility for them.

Any people depicted in stock imagery provided by Getty Images are models, and such images are being used for illustrative purposes only. Certain stock imagery © Getty Images.

Scripture taken from the King James Version of the Bible.

ISBN: 978-1-6657-2167-7 (sc)
ISBN: 978-1-6657-2168-4 (e)

Library of Congress Control Number: 2022906852

Print information available on the last page.

Archway Publishing rev. date: 05/24/2022

Contents

Preface

Thirty Years Down the Road Less Traveled

Community is a road often not taken. True community, like life, is difficult. It is hard, in part, because it requires so much unlearning and letting go, but it is worth the effort. In our acquisitive world focused on accumulating more resources, more knowledge, more power, more competitive advantage, it is counterintuitive to consider that less is more, and that unlearning is as important as learning. Unlearning necessitates letting go of the familiar and safe mental and emotional habits that keep us running on automatic pilot. Unlearning forces us to check our emotional and perceptual default settings to see if they are still valid and to go through the unnerving process of resetting them when we realize they are outmoded. Unlearning makes me question whether much of what I am certain about is wrong or deluded. Unlearning is uncomfortable, it's disorienting, and it makes me feel vulnerable. Questioning oneself causes uncertainty, which can trigger confusion and humility. Seeking community makes me less of a fortress and more of a permeable membrane as I am affected by and changed by others.

As the classic story goes, in the early ninth century, the scholar Tokusan visited Zen Master Ryutan to add to his vast knowledge of the dharma. At one point, Ryutan refilled his guest's teacup but kept pouring after the cup was full. Tea spilled out and ran over the table. "Stop! The cup is full," said Tokusan.

"Exactly," said Master Ryutan. "You are like this cup; you are full of ideas. You come and ask for teaching, but your cup is full; I can't put anything in. Before I can teach you, you'll have to empty your cup."

Of course, everyone knows that the earth is round. Try imagining that it is flat. Or that the sun revolves around the earth. In the 1800s, use of leeches to treat the cause of most diseases—excess blood—was state-of-the-art medicine. In the realm of human relationships, communications, and behavior, vast numbers of people are still using the equivalent of circa 1981 floppy disks and the MS-DOS operating system to navigate contemporary life. The system keeps crashing, but we keep rebooting in the hope that it will work.

Only in retrospect are obsolete mental models obvious, even ridiculous. So how does one question, recognize, empty out, and replace unexamined assumptions and mental models when they first begin to act up and cause problems? First and foremost, I cannot do this alone. It takes me colliding into something or someone to wake me up, to bring into my awareness that something is amiss. It also takes a willingness to let others in, to be altered, sometimes to be hurt, to be a new self, to be improved by others. I suspect there are many ways to accomplish this sort of awakening, but the one I know the best is community building.

I was called to community from an early age. My parents were chemists and devoted Unitarian Universalists, so my exposure to experimentation, the principles of inclusion, working without much direction or structure, and the necessity to find my own way began in childhood. It wasn't until I had learned about Catholicism from my friends that I realized that being raised as a Unitarian was anything but the norm.

My best friend, Sharon, explained what it meant to be Catholic: "So, let's suppose that I kiss my boyfriend, which is a sin, then go to confession, and then get hit by lightning and die. I'll go right to heaven."

That seemed both amazing and ridiculous. So I asked my dad to explain to me what Unitarians believe.

His answer: "What do you believe?"

I tried again by rewording my question, only to receive the same response. After several more unsuccessful attempts to learn the Unitarian doctrine, I got it. Faith was not something to follow and conform to, but a quest. Being a Unitarian seemed to be much harder than being a Catholic. At that moment, I realized I was not expected to follow a prescribed path or fulfill my parents' expectations for me. The only ground rule that seemed certain was my education. I recall a teary evening as a five-year-old, dragging my beloved Papa Bear downstairs. Sobbing, I asked my parents, "Can I take Papa Bear to college with me?"

My career as a budding scientist lasted my first semester at Indiana University in Bloomington. I hated chemistry. On a fluke—or was it? —I enrolled in a film course in the Comparative Literature department for the second semester and found a home. The Comp Lit professors were an eclectic, multidisciplinary crew of people who didn't quite belong in a single tract. It became clear to me that I wanted to learn how to learn, not find a profession. During my junior year, I wandered beyond the campus into the community and began volunteering at Middleway House—a crisis center for people who had dropped LSD and were freaking out. One door opened up two more, so by the time I was beginning my master's degree—in comparative literature—I, too, was running on multiple tracts, juggling my academic life and a roll-your-own job working for the newly elected mayor, a thirty-one-year-old freshly minted lawyer. Every day was thrilling, challenging, and filled with more learning and unlearning. A handful of us—all under thirty—were running city government and making it up as we went along. One of my favorite sayings became, "If red doesn't work, try blue. If blue doesn't work, try green." And so on. By admitting that I did not know, I learned how to create programs to serve the community. I figured out how to write successful grant proposals. I was exposed to a master of facilitation long before it had become a common practice. I learned about myself through personal growth experiences—the Est training, meditation retreats, and encounter groups.

The first grant proposal I developed in 1972 was for a "Weekend Community for Youth," funded by the Lily Endowment for several years. Without realizing it at the time, these paths were leading me down the road to learning about the life of a community builder. Gradually, I began doing some consulting, and by 1978, it became a more than full-time consulting business, primarily working with groups all over the country.

As I facilitated groups using some basic guidelines, I began to notice the changes that took place in the group when individuals had an opportunity to air their feelings freely without judgment, openly question their working assumptions and mental models, and be heard by others. Even in problem-solving and product planning sessions, the same pivotal shift kept occurring. When they happened, these group awakenings always seemed magical. The shift almost always happened, but I wasn't sure why or how. It wasn't until I heard Dr. M. Scott Peck speak, just before *The Different Drum* was published in 1987, that I had words for what I experienced over and over in these group experiences. In his lecture, Dr. Peck mentioned the Foundation for Community Encouragement (FCE) and the community building process. I was ecstatic and finally had some words to describe my experiences. There were other folks out there doing similar work.

Without knowing what to call it, I had been doing the work of community building. It took another couple of years to connect with FCE and attend my first workshop. I remember it as being an enlightening and powerful experience. In comparison to workshops I attended later, I would rate my first workshop a 3 or 4 on a scale of 10 in terms of the intensity of the sense of community. In the workshop, we did two days of community building followed by a more traditional workshop to understand and integrate what had happened in the community building segment. The next day, when asked whether the group had "reached community," one of the facilitators, after a thoughtful pause, responded this way: "Well, in this group, community kind up came up and kissed us on the check. In contrast, in the first workshop I attended, it was full, deep-throat orgasm." At that point, I began a deliberate journey down the road less traveled.

From that point in 1988, community building has been the single-most influential and enduring force in my life. For seventeen of those years, I worked with and was friends with Scotty and his wife, Lily, until his death in 2005. I have attended or facilitated workshops I would rate a 1 or 2, those I would rate an 11, and everything in between. Each one has generated abundant learning about other people, myself, love, spirituality, how groups evolve, and the essential element of emptiness. Using the principles and practices learned in community building as a way of life can set in motion an alternative culture, one that is devoid of violence, hatred, and oppression. Through these principles and practices, these harmful mindsets and behaviors can be unlearned and replaced with the capacity for mutual respect, compassion, and appreciation for all types of diversity.

Although *Building True Community: Thirty Years Down the Road Less Traveled* has been under construction for decades, it is no accident that I chose 2020 AD (After Donald) as the point to declare a thirty-year-work-in-progress complete enough to let it go. Since *The Different Drum* was written more than thirty years ago, community building has occurred on five continents, but relatively little has been written or published about the process. Admittedly, anyone who has experienced community building has a hard time trying to describe its complexity. Somehow, it seems wrong for such a gift sit on a shelf in the dark simply because it's difficult to wrap.

In the aftermath of the US election of 2016 and the challenges of living in COVID times, I felt an undeniable sense of urgency to reintroduce community building principles and practices to a broader public in light of our backslide into damaging patterns that emerge during times of societal division, isolation, and chaos. As Charles Dickens began in writing of another tumultuous era, "It was the best of times, it was the worst of times … it was the season of Light, it was the season of Darkness."

As I write this preface, I am still recovering from the Trump era and a prolonged period of daily doses of events and actions, words, and deeds that so perfectly demonstrated what this book is *not* about. For this is a book that is *not* about arrogance, or deception, or hubris, or assault, or fakeness, or factions, or self-righteousness, or exclusion, or mocking, or impulsivity, or deflection, or grudges, or walls, or inciting violence.

It *is* a book about a pathway out of the chaos and harm that results from living without a sense of community with others and without experiencing the glory of what it means to be human. It is, as my friend Scott Peck observed, the road less traveled, and that has made all the difference. I am grateful for the kick in the butt that the reality of pandemic life in 2020 gave me so that I finally decided to act on the ancient advice, "it is better to light a candle than curse the darkness."

Introduction

Is it possible to uncover the unconscious, deeply ingrained mental and emotional patterns that have become hardwired in us? Can old wounds and trauma be healed? Is it possible to bridge the divides that keep us separate and isolated from each other, in conflict with and harming each other? Can we begin with small steps to dismantle the ways people are routinely violated and oppressed? Can we learn how to disarm ourselves and rediscover the glory of being human?

The short answer to these questions is yes. The rest of the book outlines the long answer, with an extensive explanation of how to tap into a force that is omnipresent yet rarely experienced by people. The aim of *Building True Community* is to make the principles and practices that can create community accessible to everyone who chooses to do the personal, inner work and make external changes in our society and culture. By stepping onto the path to true community, through learning and unlearning, you will discover how to deepen and restore relationships, resolve conflicts, and experience the freedom to be your authentic, best self. By building community and experiencing a sense of community, the process can serve as both a resource and a responsibility. You will learn that it is possible to rewire your brain by developing what neuroscientist and psychiatrist Dr. Daniel Siegel calls "mindsight," the ability to dissolve fixed mental perceptions that reinforce the "optical delusion" of our separateness.

Like gravity or any other force in the universe, community has been around forever. Sir Isaac Newton is credited with the discovery of gravity by offering proof of its existence. Once named as a force with laws, gravity could be harnessed rather than being a mystery.

Similarly, the laws of community can enable people to experience and benefit from this powerful and life-giving force accessible to everyone.

In many ways, the journey to discovering a sense of community is an arduous one because it demands that individuals change deeply ingrained habits and ways of thinking. To tap into the power of community, people must directly confront what keeps the protections and divides in place that separate people and lead to conflict. Violence would not exist without fear of the unknown and fear of the other. If being truthful, authentic, and open becomes more the norm than being righteous, blaming, judging, and exercising power over others, the walls between and within people, communities, organizations, and nations would be porous and able to be dismantled. But as a human being, it seems extremely difficult to give up making oneself right and others wrong. It is uncomfortable, even painful, to admit to being fearful and vulnerable. Perhaps the most difficult of all is to own up to the consequences of abusing power. Like the golden rule, do unto others as you would have them do unto you, it is easier said than done. Community building is hard work.

Paradoxically—and community is full of paradoxes—the experience of community is easy in that the most critical ingredient is the capacity to empty oneself. Learning to be an active community builder involves learning how to unlearn and let go of barriers. For a moment, imagine what your life, your family, your workplace, and the groups you interact with would be like if people consistently were able to

- communicate with authenticity (be real with each other),
- deal with difficult issues (instead of avoiding them),
- relate with love and respect (rather than hurting each other),
- seek, welcome, and affirm diversity (of all kinds),
- bridge differences with integrity (so that all are satisfied with decisions and the process),
- acknowledge our human frailties (as a source for compassion),

- take responsibility for our actions and make amends where possible (reconciliation is always possible), and
- practice forgiveness for ourselves and others (forgiveness is a choice).

It all starts with you. As Gandhi so wisely stated, "Be the change you wish to see in the world."

Overview of the Book

Building True Community is structured in four parts: Basics, Building True Community, Application, and Connections.

The first chapter addresses the question, "Why now?" The short answer—individual and collective isolation, trauma, violence, and pain. Despite advancements in many areas, as human beings, we continue to engage in ways of being with each other that result in separation, harm, prejudice, exclusion, conflict, and broken relationships. I return to where *The Road Less Traveled* began, with Scott Peck's blinding flash of the obvious that "Life is difficult," and summarize the underpinnings of a culture of violence that thrives on chaos. Like others before me, I raise the question of whether these forms of oppression that permeate day-to-day life are an inevitable part of the human condition.

The second chapter eavesdrops on a community building circle as a way of introducing the community building model. I present it from the perspective of a first-time community builder as she moves through the ups and downs of the experience. Participants and circumstances, while realistic, are not real. One of the critical community building guidelines is confidentiality, so I drew from my personal experiences in hundreds of workshops to provide a fictionalized taste of community building.

The third chapter explores the community building model, dynamics that occur during the stages of the group process, and the underlying principles and conditions that make a sense of community possible. It also details the specific skills and practices learned through the community building process that can be applied outside the circle.

The fourth chapter focuses on the critical role of the facilitators in creating the conditions in which community can take root and flourish. In contrast to other forms of facilitation, the role of the community building facilitators is to remove controls and imposed structure so that the group can self-organize its way into community. Interventions that facilitate movement toward community are also explored.

The fifth chapter explores how the stages of community play out in daily life. The sixth chapter addresses the core competencies needed to integrate community building practices into our relationships, families, workplaces, and society. Chapter 7 explores the roots or genealogy of community and point to the times, places, and people who explored or sought to describe the phenomenon of true community—some by using the term, others by describing the experience. I also review the forms of community that influenced the community building model as described in *The Different Drum*. In the final chapter, I summarize how developments in science may offer explanations of why community building works so predictably.

Finally, the last section provides a bibliography for use by practitioners, participants in community building, and facilitators.

As a note, I have struggled throughout the writing process to determine how to refer to M. Scott Peck, MD. My options were Scott Peck, M. Scott Peck, MD, Peck, Dr. Peck, or Scotty. On one hand, I want to honor his credentials as a scientist, physician, and psychiatrist. On the other hand, I knew him as "Scotty" for seventeen years. My imperfect solution is to use multiple terms, depending on the context. When I refer to his writings, I refer to him as either M. Scott Peck, MD, or Dr. Peck. In instances where I am describing aspects of his life, a personal interaction or conversation, I will refer to him as Scotty. The intention underlying this solution to be as authentic as possible—not to exclude others.

PART 1
BASICS

Why Now?

> *All change, even very large and powerful change, begins when a few people start talking with one another about some things they care about.*
> —*Turning to One Another*, Margaret Wheatley

Troubled Times

What good is love and peace on earth
When it's exclusive?
Where's the truth in the written word
If no one reads it?
A new day dawning
Comes without warning
So don't think twice
We live in troubled times.

—Green Day

We are living in troubled times. Although every era faces its own challenges, historians will likely look back at the first half of the twenty-first century as a pivotal time in human history. Our divides are deep and growing deeper each day.

Since the beginning of the new millennium, the range and frequency of trouble have intensified. We have experienced major movement in society's tectonic plates, as terrorism has escalated around the world. On 9/11, the US's supposed immunity to terrorism ended. Subsequent attacks by foreign and homegrown terrorists escalated, along with jihadist-inspired attacks abroad. Mass shootings are becoming commonplace. Regardless of the inspiration, what the attacks have in common is the intentional use of violence in public places against innocent victims. Hearing the names of cities—Newtown, Columbine, Aurora, San Bernardino, Orlando, Paris, Nice, Brussels, Las Vegas, Dayton, El Paso—immediately brings an association with mass killings.

Concurrently, the oppressive forces of racism, sexism, classism, homophobia, and xenophobia are enjoying new popularity. Our divides are wider and deeper on political, racial, economic, and cultural fronts, as hate and extremist groups grow and flourish. In the aftermath of a white police officer's murder of a black man, George Floyd, amid the COVID-19 pandemic, protests for social justice spread across the world from Minneapolis to the Middle East and beyond. The real threat of nuclear war, dormant for more than half a century, has taken center stage.

A Culture of Violence

We live in a culture of violence, one of the primary causes of trauma. Trauma and violence are now recognized as public health issues. Today, violence results in more than 1.5 million people being killed each year, and many more suffer nonfatal injuries and chronic health consequences as a result of suicide attempts, interpersonal violence (youth violence, intimate partner violence, child abuse, elder abuse, and sexual violence), and collective violence (war and other forms of armed conflict). Overall, violence is among the leading causes of death worldwide for people aged fifteen to forty-four years.

The primary force at work in violence is the will to dominate, which allows the spirit of destruction to take root in all corners of life. The more violence becomes the norm, the more we are numbed to it and its effects. Violence is any behavior involving physical force intended to hurt, damage, or kill someone or something. However, violence is not limited to physical action, as both speech and thoughts can be violent, traumatic, and harmful.

More subtle forms of violence are less obvious. All come from the root of exercising power over others. Disrespect, malicious gossip, hostility, name-calling, arrogance, being judgmental, and all "isms" (racism, sexism, ageism, etc.) assume that someone else is "less than." These forms of violence may not be conscious efforts to harm another, but people are hurt every day in small ways that build over time. In some cases, the energy required to stand up to violent captors is so immense that traumatized people develop strong emotional bonds with those who harass, beat, threaten, abuse, or intimidate them as a defense mechanism—also known as the Stockholm syndrome. Emotional injury can even lead to death by suicide, as evidenced by the growing number of young people who commit suicide because of cyberbullying.

At earlier stages in human evolution, violence and threats of violence served our species well. The threat of violence has provided a way to survive and adapt. As humans, we are still hardwired with the genetic wisdom built into our brains that activates chemicals that prepare us for fight or flight in the face of danger or a threat to bodily harm. Perhaps there will be a time when the part of the brain that triggers response to danger will become a vestigial organ like the appendix, but given human history, that time is in the very distant future. Aggression, at its root, is a means of protection for our group, our young, our resources, our territory, and the dominance of our way of life. Without even realizing it, a person can adopt a "hurt or be hurt" response to others.

Fear is the trigger for enemy formation—the process of perceiving "the other" as a threat. The human nervous system is hardwired through a fight-or-flight mechanism to respond to fear by producing increased levels of stress hormones; elevating heart rate, blood pressure, and respiration levels; and redirecting the blood flow away from the brain's frontal cortex to the amygdala, a part of the brain's limbic system responsible for emotions and survival instincts. As humans evolved, preparing to do battle or run from saber-toothed tigers morphed into the impulse to respond similarly to an emotional, psychological, or even ideological threat. It is not hard to see how easily a simple disagreement can trigger the fear response, advance to alienation, and escalate to conflict and violence. Violence is rooted in the same attitudes that generate the walls we build as human beings. Some walls are physical, but most are emotional and psychological. These divides are constructed of fear of the unknown—anything or anyone that is different—and the need to be right. Along with the instinct of self-preservation and distrust of the other, self-righteousness easily leads to force against the enemy. Most violence begins with thoughts, then words, then actions.

To have a difference with others is different from disrespecting them. Disrespect involves holding a contrary point of view but also a feeling that one is better than or above the other and that it is acceptable to put down, chastise, or demean the other via words or actions. Disrespect can be deliberate, but more often it is unconscious, ingrained, and infused with an individual's beliefs and values. At a societal level, it is the host of isms that reflect whole belief systems—racism, sexism, ageism—that are oppressive as instruments. The bottom line is that an individual or group as a whole is less than. As fear accumulates, as hatred festers, as self-righteousness hardens, attitudes and beliefs are expressed in words. For some, words escalate into physical violence—all in an attempt to obliterate others and their differences.

Trauma and Violence: Public Health Issues

In 1979, the Centers for Disease Control and Prevention (CDC) first identified violence as one of fifteen priority public health issues for the nation, but just forty years ago, violence and health were not perceived as related in any way. Studies on adverse childhood experiences (ACEs) reveal that most Americans have at least one traumatic ACE; people with four ACEs—including living with an alcoholic parent, experiencing racism or bullying, witnessing violence outside the home, enduring physical abuse, and losing a parent to divorce—have a huge risk of adult onset of chronic health problems such as heart disease, cancer, diabetes, suicide, and alcoholism. The initial trauma study conducted by the CDC and Kaiser Permanente revealed that two-thirds of the seventeen thousand study participants experienced at least one traumatic ACE and more than one in five reported more than three ACEs. ACEs are stressful or traumatic events that can have lasting, negative effects on health and well-being. Examples include emotional, physical, and sexual abuse; neglect; parental divorce; witnessing violence; living in a family with substance abuse; or incarceration of a parent or guardian. Widely recognized as groundbreaking, the study revealed the significant prevalence of trauma and established a definite correlation between the number of experiences and negative health and well-being outcomes in adulthood. Bernie Siegel, MD, bestselling author of *Love, Medicine and Miracles*, summed it up: "I have become convinced that our number one public health issue is childhood."

A wide range of public health practitioners, researchers, and institutes continue the quest to understand the roots of violence and develop strategies to prevent its occurrence. Their experience and the scientific studies they have conducted clearly demonstrate that violence and trauma are preventable, and their impact can be reduced, in the same way that public health efforts have prevented and reduced tobacco use, pregnancy-related complications, workplace injuries, infectious diseases, and illness resulting from contaminated food and water in many parts of the world. If heart disease, cancer, and stroke can be prevented through behavioral modifications, why cannot violence be prevented? As long as there has been violence, there have also been systems—religious, philosophical, legal, and communal—that have grown up to prevent or limit it. None has been completely successful, but all have made their contribution to this defining mark of civilization.

Even though violence has always been present, the world does not have to accept it as an inevitable part of the human condition. The American Psychological Association and the National Academy of Science now concur that violence is in large part a socially constructed, learned behavior. Socially constructed, learned behaviors are not inevitable. The factors that contribute to violent responses—whether they are factors of attitude and behavior or related to larger social, economic, political, and cultural conditions—can be changed. Like tackling any other major issues like health disparities and health equity, it is no easy task. It is unlikely that individual, biologically driven urges—anger, frustration, aggression—can be eliminated, but by creating a different set of social conditions, building new competencies, and creating new neural pathways in the brain, these impulses can be drastically reduced.

We are witnessing a tipping point in contemporary culture as women, and some men, are speaking out to end sexual assault and harassment. The movement, known as #MeToo on social media, was prompted by the public revelations of sexual misconduct by Hollywood mogul Harvey Weinstein. After years of women's stories being dismissed in most cases, suddenly within a matter of months, the post-Weinstein momentum gained sufficient steam to topple a still-growing list of politicians, Hollywood celebrities, business executives, and other men in positions of power who had engaged in predatory behavior that was taken for granted as being acceptable. There will be exceptions, but going forward, anyone considering an aggressive sexual advance will think twice before acting. Finally, women who have been victims are telling their stories and being believed. Perpetrators are facing real consequences. This pervasive, oppressive, and violent cultural norm is changing forever.

Environmental Violence

> *To corrupt or destroy the natural environment is an act of violence not only against the earth but also against those who are dependent on it, including ourselves.*
>
> —Wendell Berry

When we think of violence, it typically concerns other human beings. Environmental violence may be the most urgent and pervasive form of violence that affects every living thing on our planet. Each time there is a mass shooting, we are confronted with a dramatic, visible, immediate extinction of human life. Bandy X. Lee, an expert in psychiatry in society, spoke to this vital issue in a 2018 post in *Psychology Today*:

> Given the crucial importance of the environment to human survival, the disproportionate lack of concern in the face of scientific warnings of catastrophic changes, especially when humans have been instigators of these changes, may amount to collective suicide.
>
> When we speak of *environmental violence*, we are referring to the direct damage to the environment by humans, but also the violent response from the natural world as a result of human degradation of the environment and the violence humans do to one another because of their effects on the climate. We need to recognize that damage to the environment is a human issue, for our survival is at stake, along with that of other species; the planet itself will continue. Our

apparent unconcern about it, demonstrated by the major pushback we see against changing our behavior to rectify the problem, is an indication of how much we need a global and societal psychiatry that can help interpret and treat the pathological tendencies of humankind as a whole.

"A Willing Suspension of Disbelief"

The utter absurdity of the proposition that the world—or my own community—could be nonviolent may be intriguing enough to cause people to begin questioning the inevitability of violence. In the words of the poet Samuel Taylor Coleridge, consider the possibility "with a willing suspension of disbelief."

As I witnessed the aftermath of the school shootings at Newtown, Connecticut, before Christmas of 2012, I decided that I could no longer be the sole beneficiary of all that I had learned through community building. On that tragic day, twenty children and seven adults, including the shooter, lost their lives through an unthinkable act of violence. For twenty-five years, I lived just fifteen minutes away from Newtown in Connecticut's Fairfield County, so the tragedy hit close to home. As I watched the news coverage nonstop for several days, much as I did after 9/11, I watched the small town overflow with mountains of stuffed animals and flowers sent from individuals all over the world. Bouquets of balloons floated over candles spread like a blanket over the frozen ground. Notes, decorations, angels on sticks, wreaths, photos, ribbons, and toys were everywhere. Forced to deal with warehouses full of items, officials requested that the public refrain from sending more gifts.

I saw the deluge of gifts as a collective expression of grief about the massacre and as a way of doing something concrete to relieve the suffering and grief, albeit symbolic. If only the thousands of caring people had another way to turn their empathy and compassion into concrete action, that might prevent future acts of violence! Rather than sending gifts, perhaps individuals could begin to take preventative action in their own lives and workplaces.

The premise of *Building True Community* is that it is possible to dismantle the culture of violence and replace it with the ways of nonviolence, one individual, one relationship, one group, and one community at a time. At times like ours, the principles and practices of community building may seem naïve and an improbable antidote to the violent chaos erupting unpredictably around the world. Yet, the widespread spontaneous response to the Paris attacks was to light a candle. Messages in chalk on Paris streets called for love. One public official, in response to the Las Vegas mass killing—the worst in US history—summed it all up: "We have to change the culture of living in fear of the other."

Life is better in the circle.
—Joe DeMars

A Taste of Community

I spoke to a friend recently who had attended a community building workshop. She mentioned trying to explain the experience to her husband. She had a hard time doing so. As I listened to her frustration, I recalled the countless times I had attempted to tell another person about the experience, only to end up saying, "I guess you had to be there." The following is a fictional community building experience. None of the participants are real people. But they could be. And their stories could be real. It is just a taste of what an experience could be and a window into being in the circle.

A Community Building Experience: Day One

One by one, people check in at the desk outside the large meeting room. A stack of paste-on name tags and a handful of markers are scattered next to the sign-in sheet. I get my name tag, wondering for a minute whether to write both my first and last names and whether to place it on the left or right. I notice that some people are quiet; others are talking nervously. I don't feel like talking to anyone else. I have too much on my mind now. Inside the meeting space, thirty-five chairs are set up in a circle. Several boxes of tissues are on the floor near the chairs. I pick a spot and settle in.

The circle begins to fill in, and I scan the room. It looks like we will have an interesting group, given the mix of people—some young adults, middle-aged folks, and a handful of seniors. I notice that the group is quite the melting pot. Three women and a man come into the room together, speaking Spanish, laughing, and head for the coffee pot. About a third of the group is African American, and two women are dressed in African garb. I notice an older Asian man and a middle-aged Asian woman. It is a couple of minutes before nine, and a man and a woman come in, separate, and sit across from each other in the circle. The woman is carrying a three-ring binder.

All but three of the chairs are filled. The woman with the notebook announces that the workshop is going to begin. The buzz subsides.

"My name is Janet, and Paul and I will be your facilitators." The man across the circle raises his hand and nods. "Our task this weekend is to build community with the people here in this circle. To get started, we have a bit of information to share with you about the work of community building and some guidelines for the work we are about to begin. Would someone be willing to read the Founding Dream?" Janet points to a laminated chart posted on the wall.

After a pause, a large man, about forty, speaks up. His name tag says "Leroy." "I'll do it. 'There is a yearning in the heart for peace. Because of the wounds and rejections we have received in past relationships, we are frightened by the risk of disarming ourselves. In our fear, we discount the dream of authentic community as merely visionary. But there are rules by which people can come back together, and by which the old wounds can be healed. It is the mission of FCE to teach these rules, to make hope real again, to make the vision actually manifest in a world which has almost forgotten the glory of what it means to be human.'"

"Thanks, Leroy," says Janet. "And would someone else be willing to read the mission statement?"

This time, the Asian woman responds, "I will; my name's Yumiko. 'FCE encourages people, in a fragmented world, to discover new and better ways of being together. Living, learning, and teaching the principles of community, FCE serves as a catalyst for individuals, groups, and organizations to communicate with authenticity; relate with love and respect; deal with difficult issues; seek, honor, and affirm diversity; bridge differences with integrity; acknowledge our human frailties; take responsibility for our actions and make amends where possible; and practice forgiveness for ourselves and others. FCE's approach encourages tolerance of ambiguity, the experience of discovery, and the tension between holding on and letting go. In our work to empower others, we remember our reliance upon a Spirit within and beyond ourselves."

"Thank you, Yumiko. My name is Paul, and Janet and I will be your facilitators. As facilitators, we are only guides. No one is more or less responsible for building a sense of community in this group. In a community, everyone in the group is a leader.

"I am going to review the guidelines we will use. Some of the guidelines are simple, and others are more complex. The first guideline is to wear a name tag and to use your name before you speak. This is for a couple of reasons. In a group this large, it helps everyone learn each other's names, but when I use my name, it also helps me own what I say.

"Please be on time for each session. We have a limited amount of time to build community, so please honor the time schedule.

"The next guideline is to be present. Be emotionally present to each other.

"It is also important to avoid generalities and to speak personally, using 'I' statements instead of 'you' or 'we' statements. Let me give you an example. A statement like 'Divorce is a terrible thing' implies that everyone has the same experience. On the other hand, if I say, 'For me, my divorce was one of the most liberating experiences of my life,' I am only speaking for myself.

"The next guideline is to be inclusive. Exclusivity is the enemy of community, and it comes in two forms. First, I can exclude others. I can exclude you in my heart and mind, and you may never know it. The other way is to exclude yourself. Suppose I am uncomfortable with what is going on in the group. So, I just quietly take myself out of the group—of course I'm still sitting here—and start observing you. When I find myself doing this sort of checking out, one way back in is simply to acknowledge it. For example, 'I've been sitting here for the last few minutes watching as if I'm outside the circle, so I'd like to bring myself back in.'

"Participation in the workshop can be either verbal or nonverbal. There is no requirement to speak.

"We encourage you to speak when you are moved and to not speak when you aren't moved. I can't tell you what it might be like for you when you are moved to speak because each person experiences it differently. Pay attention to your inner stirrings, and when you find yourself moved to speak, please do so.

"We also ask you to hang in for the duration. Throughout the course of our time together, there may be difficult periods of frustration, depression, even despair. Please do your best to stay the course. There are no chains or shackles, however, and if you find that you must leave, please let one of us know.

"Express displeasure in the group, not outside the room. That doesn't mean that you cannot talk outside the room about the workshop, but please bring your issues or concerns back to the group.

"The last guideline is to respect confidentiality. What is said here stays here. This is such an important part of the process that I'm going to go around the room and make brief eye contact with each of you, and please indicate your consent."

Paul's eyes moved around the circle, connecting with everyone until they nodded or said yes. Most of the people nodded.

"My name is Janet. There are a few other items we'd like to cover. You may notice that either Paul or I may take some notes. These are notes about the process, which we may use to reflect on the group's process. We won't be available during the breaks, because we use that time to meet and discuss the progress of the group. We will take breaks at about the midpoint of the morning and afternoon, and we will break at lunch for an hour. However, if you need to use the restroom at other times, you are free to do so. Please just pay attention to what is going on in the group and be sensitive about the timing. Paul, have I missed anything?"

"No, that's it."

"Any procedural questions?" Silence. "We will begin our first session with a story, followed by three minutes of silence, and perhaps someone will be moved to speak."

Janet opens her binder.

"The story is called 'The Rabbi's Gift.'"

"The story concerns a monastery that had fallen upon hard times. It was once a great order, but as a result of waves of antimonastic persecution in the seventeenth and eighteenth centuries and the rise of secularism in the nineteenth, all its branch houses were lost, and it had become decimated to the extent that there were only five monks left in the decaying mother house: the abbot and four others, all over seventy in age. Clearly, it was a dying order.

"In the deep woods surrounding the monastery, there was a little hut that a rabbi from a nearby town occasionally used for a hermitage. Through their many years of prayer and contemplation, the old monks had become a bit psychic, so they could always sense when the rabbi was in his hermitage. 'The rabbi is in the woods, the rabbi is in the woods again,' they would whisper to each other. As he agonized over the imminent death of his order, it occurred to the abbot at one such time to visit the hermitage and ask the rabbi if he could offer any advice that might save the monastery.

"The rabbi welcomed the abbot into his hut. But when the abbot explained the purpose of his visit, the rabbi could only commiserate with him. 'I know how it is,' he exclaimed. 'The spirit has gone out of the people. It is the same in my town. Almost no one comes to the synagogue anymore.' So the old abbot and the old rabbi wept together. Then they read parts of the Torah and quietly spoke of deep things. The time came when the abbot had to leave. They embraced each other. "It has been a wonderful thing that we should meet after all these years,' the abbot said, 'but I have still failed in my purpose for coming here. Is there nothing you can tell me, no piece of advice you can give me that would help me save my dying order?'

"'No, I am sorry,' the rabbi responded. 'I have no advice to give. The only thing I can tell you is that the Messiah is one of you.'

"When the abbot returned to the monastery, his fellow monks gathered around him to ask, 'Well what did the rabbi say?' 'He couldn't help,' the abbot answered. 'We just wept and read the Torah together. The only thing he did say, just as I was leaving, it was something cryptic, that the Messiah is one of us. I don't know what he meant.'

"In the days and weeks and months that followed, the old monks pondered this and wondered whether there was any possible significance to the rabbi's words. The Messiah is one of us? Could he possibly have meant one of us monks here at the monastery? If that's the case, which one? Do you suppose he meant the abbot? Yes, if he meant anyone, he probably meant Father Abbot. He has been our leader for more than a generation. On the other hand, he might have meant Brother Thomas. Certainly Brother Thomas is a holy man. Everyone knows that Thomas is a man of light. Certainly he could not have meant Brother Elred! Elred gets crotchety at times. But come to think of it, even though he is a thorn in people's sides, when you look back on it, Elred is virtually always right. Often very right. Maybe the rabbi did mean Brother Elred. But surely not Brother Phillip. Phillip is so passive, a real nobody. But then, almost mysteriously, he has a gift for somehow always being there when you need him. He just magically appears by your side. Maybe Phillip is the Messiah. Of course the rabbi didn't mean me. He couldn't possibly have meant me. I'm just an ordinary person. Yet supposing he did? Suppose I am the Messiah? O God, not me. I couldn't be that much for you, could I?

"As they contemplated in this manner, the old monks began to treat each other with extraordinary respect, on the off chance that one among them might be the Messiah. And on the off chance that each monk himself might be the Messiah, they began to treat themselves with extraordinary respect.

"Because the forest in which it was situated was beautiful, it so happened that people still occasionally came to visit the monastery to picnic on its tiny lawn, to wander along some of its paths, even now and then to go into the dilapidated chapel to meditate. As they did so, without even being conscious of it, they sensed the aura of extraordinary respect that now began to surround the five old monks and seemed to radiate out from them and permeate the atmosphere of the place. There was something strangely attractive, even compelling, about it. Hardly knowing why, they began to come back to the monastery more frequently to picnic, to play, to pray. They began to bring their friends to show them this special place. And their friends brought their friends.

"Then it happened that some of the younger men who came to visit the monastery started to talk more and more with the old monks. After a while, one asked if he could join them. Then another. And another. So within a few years, the monastery had once again become a thriving order and, thanks to the rabbi's gift, a vibrant center of light and spirituality in the realm."

Janet closes the binder and looks up. "Let's have three minutes of silence, and I'll let you know when the time is over." She glances at her watch.

I ponder the story during the silence, which seemed very long and a bit odd. The monk I identify with was the last one, the one who found it hard to accept that he might be the Messiah. I think about how rarely I see faults in others but see them easily in myself. My friend, Bob, always teases me about my glass always being half-full. It's always half-empty for him. I feel nervous, but I don't think that equates with being "moved." More silence. Finally, Janet says, "Three minutes is up."

That's it? I ask myself. *That doesn't give us much to work with.* I look around the room, and everyone else looks as confused as I am. More silence. *It feels so, so awkward. Maybe I should say something about the story. I did think about it. No, I would be doing that just to break the silence.*

"I'm John, and I really liked the story. I grew up Catholic, and the story reminded me of the priests in our parish and how kind they were. It seems like over the years, I've known a priest like each one in the story. I was even going to be a priest but decided against it. I liked sex too much." Subdued laughter broke the tension. "That's it for now."

More silence. *At this rate, it's going to be a very long weekend.*

"My name is Kaneesha. What I found amazing about the story was that the monks had to go outside their own community to get some answers, some help. They actually dared to go to a rabbi, of all people, to ask for advice. How often does that happen?"

"I think that happens all the time. Sorry, my name is Harvey. I am a consultant, and I'm like the rabbi—hey, I'm even Jewish. That's what we do as outside consultants. In my case, though, I have advice to give instead of a confusing and vague statement. That's why businesses seek out my firm's expertise. To tell the truth, I thought the story was pretty simplistic."

What a jerk, I think.

Harvey keeps talking. "You know, this group is too big for us to get anything done, and I don't even know anything about any of you here. Why don't we go around the room and introduce ourselves? You already know a little about me." Harvey laughs nervously.

"I'm Robert. I don't want to do that." Harvey looks crushed. He pushes his chair back a few inches.

I am not sure if I am relieved or disappointed that Robert stopped the introductions.

"Why do we need to use our names?"

"I'm Harvey. And what's your name?"

"I think that's a stupid rule. Okay. I'm Melvin."

A long, anxious silence.

"Sarah, here. I liked the story too, but I was troubled that there were no women. Don't get me wrong, I could still identify with the monks, but here we are, trying to be inclusive, and the first thing we hear is a story all about men. By the way, in case you are wondering, I am following the guideline about voicing displeasure in the group."

She has a point.

I look at my watch. *It's a few minutes after ten, and nothing is happening.* A seemingly endless stream of people elaborate more about the story, offering a dozen more interpretations. I tune them out and start counting the carpet squares inside the circle. *This is death by boredom. Maybe I will leave at the break.*

"My name is Paul, and let's take a break for fifteen minutes. We'll start again at 10:30."

People seem to rush out of the room. I sit for a minute or two, wondering what to do. I decide to give it until lunch before deciding to leave or not. *After all, it's still early in the process. And they said there might be difficult points in the process.*

I finally get up and head for the restroom. I don't feel like talking to anyone. I overhear two women talking about the process. It's clear that they have come together to the workshop and that one of them has experienced community building at another workshop.

"Just wait. This is nothing. It won't be long before all hell breaks loose. I promise you; you won't be bored then."

"Carol, I have no idea how to do this community building stuff. Those leaders aren't providing any direction at all. Aren't they supposed to do something to get the ball rolling? We don't even have any kind of an agenda. What are we supposed to talk about other than that dumb story? If anyone else brings it up after the break, I think I'm going to scream."

"Pam, I hear you. Why don't you bring those concerns back to the group? Maybe you are not the only one who has those feelings."

Their voices fade as they leave the restroom, so I can't hear Pam's response. I'm still sitting on the john, checking my email on my iPhone, and realize it's about time to start again.

When I return to the room, the facilitators have moved to different seats. Some participants are in the same seats, and others are in a different spot. I am one of the last people back in the room, and the only chairs left are one next to Harvey and one next to Paul. I don't want to sit either place, but finally sit down next to Harvey. He turns to me with a big smile and extends his hand.

"I'm Harvey," he says. "Nice to meet you."

"Yes, I know," I respond. "I'm Marie." I shake his hand out of habit.

"How did you think the first session went?" he asks. "I don't know what to think …"

"I'm Paul. Let's continue with our work. We will begin with some silence, and I will let you know when the three minutes is up."

Three very long minutes pass.

"Okay."

"My name is Pam. This is my first workshop, and I am really confused. I have a lot of judgments about the facilitators and feel really frustrated that they aren't providing any help at all. You both must know all about community, or you wouldn't be facilitators, but you are just sitting there being smug and letting us flounder. So this whole thing is starting to piss me off. It's a waste of my time. So there. I said it."

Paul and Janet make eye contact, but neither one says anything.

"I'm Phillip, and I agree with Pam."

"Marcene, here. I must be moved to speak because I feel like my heart about to jump out of my chest. All I can think about is something that was said during the first session. Harvey, I think you were being really disrespectful when you made those comments about the rabbi and about the story being simplistic ..."

"Oh, my God, I can't stand to here one more mention of that story. I'm Pam, by the way."

Marcene looks dumbstruck. She purses her lips and continues, "I'm still Marcene, and Pam, I wasn't finished. I don't appreciate being interrupted." She glares at Pam and then softens a bit. "I have never heard that story, and I was pretty close to tears at the end. I saw myself in it, not by identifying with any of the monks or the rabbi. All I heard were those little criticisms: he's crochety, he's so passive. I started to see how often I judge others quickly, without even giving them a chance. And here I am, doing it again, by thinking that you are being disrespectful, Harvey. I don't think I ever try to look equally at the good parts in a person because I'm so busy pointing out their weaknesses. Then I convince myself that it's okay because I am even more critical of myself."

Marcene pauses and then starts crying softly.

"I'm sorry. I don't know why I am getting so emotional about this. I guess I'm just feeling ashamed."

I find myself listening to Marcene, feeling a little emotional myself. She was speaking for me. Suddenly, I felt bad about thinking that Harvey was a jerk and not wanting to sit next to him. I turn to him, catch his glance, and smile at him. I guess it is my way of including him.

I realize that neither of the facilitators has responded to Pam's challenge to them. *Hmmm. I don't think I could do that. Maybe they are not supposed to respond.*

"Pam here. I want to go back to what I brought up earlier, since no one has bothered to respond," she said, thick with sarcasm.

"I'm Phillip. Pam, that's not true. I said I agreed with you."

"Well, I suppose my name is still Pam, and Phillip, you're right. You did respond, but you didn't add anything very helpful. I'm looking for some damn leadership of this group. I spent a lot of money to get here, only to find myself in one of the most frustrating and unproductive workshops I've ever attended, and believe me, I've attended quite a few." Pam crossed her arms over her chest. "Who else feels the way I do?"

In addition to Phillip, a couple of other people raise their hands, reluctantly. "See," Pam continues, "we're not the only ones, Phillip. If someone doesn't do something about this, there won't be much of a group after lunch." Her face had turned bright red, and she looks across the circle to her friend, Carol. "Carol, you talked me into coming to this with you. Is this like all the other workshops you have attended?"

Carol returns the gaze. After a few seconds, she responds, "My name is Carol. Pam, you are my dear friend. But I must be honest. I'm not moved to speak or to answer, so I'm not going to respond directly to your question. Sorry."

Whoa, that takes some guts, I think. *Go girl.*

I don't like what is going on, but it certainly isn't boring. So far, the only people I feel connected to are Marcene, now Carol and Harvey—a little bit. I want Pam to shut up.

"Okay, I'm still Melvin. What is all this business of being moved to speak? I have no idea what that means. I've never been in any kind of a workshop that has such ridiculous rules. I know you facilitators call them 'guidelines,' but they sure sound like rules to me. Be on time. Wear name tags. What if I don't want to? This is not working at all."

"Hello, everyone. My name is Edward. I've been sitting here all morning, listening to everyone. It seems to me that this is a clear case of exactly what happens in groups as they develop. The model I find most helpful was developed by Bruce Tuckman back in 1965. He calls the stages forming, storming, norming, and performing, and from all appearances, we are in the storming phase. This is all par for the course."

"Pam here. Well, Mr. Smartie Pants, why don't you lead us out of this mess?"

"I'm Edward. I will defer to the facilitators, but I suggest that we break into some smaller groups so that people can speak more freely. The optimal group size is between seven and sixteen, with twelve being ideal. We could form, let's say, three small groups. Each group could come up with some achievable goals. Paul and Janet could facilitate two of the groups, and I'd be glad to facilitate the third one, since I have quite a bit of experience."

Edward's suggestion seems reasonable to me, and after all, they said we had to figure this out ourselves. Still, the facilitators say and do nothing.

"My name is Earl. I'm having a lot of difficulty with what's going on in the group now. When Marcene spoke a while back, the feeling in the room shifted dramatically, and for a moment, I thought we were getting somewhere. I felt my own insides being stirred and seemed to be on the brink of seeing something new about myself. Then I suddenly was jerked back to questioning the facilitators and Melvin challenging the rules. All my anxiety is back."

Earl stopped, gathering his thoughts.

"But I guess I'm moved to speak. Over the last few minutes, I have started to see that I am so afraid that I'll be criticized and judged, that I can't do anything unless it's 'perfect.'" Earl gestured with his fingers, indicating air quotes. "Growing up as a kid, my father's favorite line was 'The good is the enemy of perfect. Son, it's not perfect yet. Try harder.' It wasn't until I got to college that I discovered that he was misquoting Voltaire. Voltaire's observation was other way around: perfect is the enemy of the good.' I cannot be human and be perfect, and that's beginning to be okay with me. But it is so, so hard for me to let go of being perfect all the time. I was moved to speak a couple of times earlier today, but I was afraid I wouldn't do it right. Now I'm glad I spoke, even if it doesn't make perfect sense. See, there I go again."

A gentle laughter spills into the room in response to Earl poking fun at himself. Then there is silence. The quiet seems different this time. It is comforting and gives me a chance to take in what Earl said. I stop being angry at Pam. But not for long.

"I'm Pam. Sorry, Earl, but I didn't come here to do therapy and hear about people's problems with their parents. I came here to learn about community building and how we can make our neighborhood, our city, and our country a better place to live and raise our children."

I've had it. Once again, I am drawn to Earl, but Pam diverts the group again. I start to feel like she is holding the group back with her mean-spiritedness and constant criticizing—ironically, under the guise of insisting on progress. But aren't I doing the same to her? I know it is a matter of time before I have to say something. *Am I reacting or being moved?* I still am not sure.

Kaneesha interrupts my reflection. "I'm Kaneesha. I'm here to learn about community building, too. I live in Chicago's South Side. In Chicago last year, we had 506 murders. One of those people was my son." She starts sobbing. Someone begins passing a box of tissues around the circle. Sarah, who is sitting next to her, offers Kaneesha a tissue. "Thank you. He was seventeen years old. My son wasn't in a gang. He wasn't doing drugs. He had never been in trouble. He was killed in a drive-by on his way home from school." Kaneesha's tears well up again. Then I start crying with her, for her, quite spontaneously. "I came here for two reasons. The first was to try to let go of some of the anger and grief that have taken up residence in my heart. The second reason is that I believe there has to be another way for us humans to be together." She takes a deep breath. "Thank you for listening. My burden feels a little lighter."

Wow. I can't even imagine.

"I'm Paul, and it's time to break for lunch."

Lunch at the retreat center consists of canned corn and green beans, baked chicken, iceberg lettuce with some carrot shreds, and yellow cake with coconut frosting. I take my tray to a table with some of my fellow community builders and sit down in an empty spot. Harvey and Edward are discussing gun control. Kaneesha and Robert are talking with Yumiko and another man about the HIV prevention program they work on back home.

"May I join you?" I ask. I sit down next to Melissa. After such an intense morning, it's a relief to eat canned corn and eavesdrop on a conversation about gun control. Melissa asks me where I'm from, and we exchange some banalities about travel to the location.

"Yumiko, you haven't said anything in the workshop yet," I comment. "Lloyd, you either."

Lloyd looks up from his plate at me and says, "And neither have you."

Could that be true? How could I sit the entire morning and say nothing? It felt as if I was talking the whole time, but he was right. It was all in my head.

"Yeah, I guess I haven't. I thought I was moved a couple of time, but I wasn't sure, so I didn't say anything. Besides, it was hard to get a word in there for a while with Miss Pam." I shook my head.

"Sounds like you've got some issues with Pam," Yumiko observes.

She was right. Big issues. "I guess so," I reply, thinking about what she said. "Don't you?"

"No, she's just saying what a lot of other people are thinking," replies Yumiko.

Lloyd nods.

"So you guys have done this before?" I ask.

"Oh, indeed we have," says Lloyd. "Our whole organization has done community building, and if you think this is something, you should see what happens when people have history with each other. Hang in there. It's all worth it in the end. Just be patient."

It is time to start up again. I decide to give it until the end of the day.

The room looks different as I return to the circle. It seems brighter. I look up at the ceiling to see if the lights have been turned up. I sit down next to Kaneesha. She gives me a little smile.

"Hi there, Miss Marie," she says. "How are you doing?" She seems to really care how I am doing.

"Kaneesha, I am so sorry to hear about your son. My heart goes out to you." I reach over and give her a hug, which she gracefully accepts. She reaches out and holds my hand, tightly. "Miss Marie, I felt you out there with me. I saw those tears. I appreciate your kindness."

I melt. A few hours earlier, this woman was a total stranger.

"My name is Janet. Welcome back. Paul and I met after the last session, and we'd like to offer a few comments about the process. We observed that there has been some deep sharing, but the group is still solidly in chaos. The group seems to be seeking out ways to move forward, but the way out of the chaos is not through organizing ourselves into another structure. What we can tell you is that for this group to experience a sense of community, reflect on what you are holding onto that may be preventing you from connecting to each other in an authentic way. As you are moved, emptying those barriers will help us advance in our adventure in the unknown. Paul, do you have anything you'd like to add?"

"I'm Paul. No. That's it."

"We'll begin with silence, and I'll call us out," Janet says.

Three minutes pass. No one speaks for what seems like a long time, but the silence doesn't bother me. There is so much to reflect on from the morning.

"I am Daryl. I didn't have much to say this morning, but I just wanted to join the group. I have been listening to everyone and have learned a lot already. That's it for now."

"This name thing is really bothering me, but okay, my name is Justine. I think we are spending way too much time focusing on all this negativity and pain. The universe is made up of pure joy, and we all know that God is love. So I want to put a word in for giving equal time to the good things in our lives. My daughter just had her first baby, and I'm finally a grandmother. I don't see why we can't build community by sharing about our happiness."

"Pam here. Stop with the Pollyanna stuff, Justine. Haven't you heard the expression 'Life sucks and then you die'?"

Oh, no. Here we go again.

"I'm Justine. Pam, I don't find that very helpful. You seem to have a negative or sarcastic comment about everyone and everything. You are a big part of the negativity in the room. I think you'd be a lot more helpful if you just were quiet for a while. I seriously doubt that you have been moved to speak even once, even though you've had a lot to say."

Melvin jumps right in, remaining nameless. "I'm probably sounding like a broken record, but these rules are not helping."

"Justine, here. Melvin, I'm having a really hard time with you too. We are all trying our best to follow the guidelines, and you just keep questioning them and referring to them as 'rules.' You are the one who's not helping. It has nothing to do with the so-called rules. You are just getting in the way.'"

I go away again as the bickering continues, with various people in the group taking sides. It's starting to feel like a recurring nightmare. I am having a hard time staying awake and realize that if I close my eyes for a bit, people will just think I'm meditating or praying. I doze off for a few minutes until Robert nudges me. He leans over and whispers in my ear, "You were snoring, and I thought I better wake you up."

I'm horrified and embarrassed. I go over to the coffee table and grab a cup of black coffee. I'm not sure what I missed.

As I sit back down, a woman across from me in the circle stands up. She appears to be in her seventies. Her face is flushed. "I am Nancy. I must leave this group. I came here to learn peace-making, and we are doing the opposite. Sorry to all of you, but I have to take care of myself."

She walks across the room, and as soon as the door closes, Phillip jumps in. "My name is Phillip. Melvin, look what you did. You drove Nancy away."

A few people nod their heads in agreement.

"Still Melvin. C'mon, get a grip. This is a free country, and Nancy had the right to walk out. In fact, I'm thinking about it myself."

The facilitators call a break, asking us stay in silence during the break. When we return, Paul reiterates that the group seems to be reluctant to empty, adding that as soon as someone jumps into the deep water, there seems to be a retreat into chaos. He suggests that we can go deeper. This time, he indicates that he will call us into silence and that the silence will end when someone is moved to speak.

Edward breaks the silence. "I'm Edward. It has been a difficult few hours for me. I found myself licking my wounds from the morning and not knowing quite how to respond. There were so many emotions running through me—shame, anger, frustration, rejection, but most of all a deep sense of feeling so disoriented, as if some cosmic rug had been pulled out from under me. When I try to trace it back to an instant, I guess it was being called Mr. Smartie Pants by Pam."

He turns and looks directly at Pam, who is shifting uneasily in her seat.

"Pam, I imagine you were just expressing your frustration, but did you ever nail me. I've always relied on my mind to get me through. As a kid, I was a real nerd—always reading, one of the four members of the chess club, not much of a club really, because we just played chess and never talked about anything. I had a hard time making friends and got teased a lot because I was always husky, as my mom said. That was a nice way of saying fat." He paused, fighting back his emotions. "All I had going for me was my intelligence, so I excelled in school, went to an Ivy League university, went on for a doctorate, and have been a professor for the last number of years. Which brings me to this morning, when I suggested dividing up into smaller groups, and it felt totally flat. No one followed my lead. Or even commented on it. I felt invisible. And hurt. But after I sat with it for a while, I realized that

I did it to myself. Maybe for the first time, I realized that the mask I wear is the know-it-all. In that moment, I saw how I've put all the proverbial eggs in that basket, and without my intellect, I'm nothing, or at least it feels that way right now. But I'm beginning to get a peek at who I am when I don't know, and I think I like that guy a lot more. Maybe there is some hope, after all. So Pam, thanks for waking me up. You did me a kindness, whether you knew it or not."

I am stunned. *Is this the same guy who lectured the group about Tuckman and the forming storming crap?*

Pam starts to cry. "I'm Pam. I am so sorry, Edward. I didn't mean to hurt you, but as soon as I said what I did, I felt terrible. I just felt so lost and unsafe. I was being a real brat. I hate rules, and I think I was doing my best this morning to break them all."

Edward stands up and walks across the circle toward Pam. "Could you use a hug?" Pam welcomes his big arms, and two hold the embrace for a minute or so, rocking back and forth. People around the circle reach for tissues as they witness this unlikely reconciliation. They separate, and Edward holds her at arm's length.

"Thank you," he says. "I feel a bit more human." He returns to his seat.

"My name is Melvin."

Melvin pauses and looks around the circle. Then, he buries his face in his hands and begins to weep.

Much to my surprise, it seems as though I can feel his sorrow. *But I don't even know this guy, and he's been a real jerk. Why am I feeling this from him?*

The entire room is alert, waiting for his tears to subside. Finally, he begins to speak in a soft voice—in contrast to his previous gruffness.

"I'm Melvin. I didn't mean to harm anyone or make anyone leave the group, so I am sorry for what happened. I'm feeling awful about Nancy leaving. It's my fault.

"You see, rules have always been an issue for me. Growing up, my parents were busy drugging and drinking, so I didn't have many rules, other than being expected to take care of my baby brother and sister. But when my dad got drunk, he also got mad and took it out on us kids. He made me get down on my knees. Then he beat me with his belt."

Melvin paused and started to cry again. "He would yell at me, ordering me to bark. I can still hear the words: 'Bark, you dirty dog.' Over and over."

"Since I didn't know much about rules or understand them, I went along with my friends and ended up getting arrested for a burglary when I was nineteen. Boy, did have a lot of learning to do about rules when I went to prison. I was released after a six-year sentence two months ago. I'm having a hard time coming home. So rules are a loaded issue for me. Sorry, everybody. I am afraid and just want to fit in, but I guess I didn't help myself. So I guess these guidelines aren't so bad."

I reach for a tissue and see that the tissue box is being passed around the room.

Edward's and Melvin's sharing starts a chain reaction. One after another, people begin to open, drop their masks, and share about a whole range of human experiences. Occasionally, someone jumps in too quickly after someone shares in a vulnerable way. Each time, a person in the group steps in and asks that he or she wait just a moment to allow some space and time to reflect on the previous speaker. Unlike the morning, when people were critical of the process or the facilitators or gave a generous dose of advice, the group just moves on and does not get stuck dwelling on the person or what they have to say. The last part of the day flies by, and before I know if, Paul is saying that it's five o'clock and time to call it a day.

"I will ask that you are gentle with yourselves this evening," he says. "Get some rest, and take care of yourself. We have done a lot of hard work today, and it can be exhausting. Also, pay attention to your dreams. Sometimes, one or more people will have a group dream that can offer us guidance. Be well."

Given what unfolded that afternoon, there is no way I am leaving.

After the session, I eat dinner alone in my room, trying to sort out the events of the day. What a distance the group has traveled in a few short hours. I reflect on how my attitude has shifted since the beginning of the day and realize how deeply ingrained my own flight response is. Suddenly, as I work my way through a burger and fries, I see in my mind's eye an elaborate set of dominoes arranged on a large surface. Once I realize how close I came to bolting from the workshop, that first domino bumps the next one, and the whole structure falls. Flashing through my mind are all the times and places when my instinct told me to run away, either physically or emotionally. These countless times when I had one foot out the door in a relationship, a group, or an organization come to mind like flashcards. I see that my responses were triggered by feeling threatened, feeling inadequate, or being afraid of conflict. In the community building exercise, it was easier to think about leaving than facing these strangers and enduring a process that seemed like a ship without a rudder. On the other hand, I have made it through the day and found myself able to connect with a few of the other participants.

There was that moment with Kaneesha, when I felt her sorrow and was so touched that I wept with her. And my negative views of Harvey and Edward had softened a bit. After I finish my dinner, I walk to the hospitality room, which is open for participants who wish to gather after the workshop.

The room is buzzing. About twenty people from workshop are gathered in pairs or small clusters—a refreshing change from the large circle. Kaneesha, who is sitting with John, spots me right away, waves, and then motions for me to join them. I am happy to see her.

"How are you doing, Kaneesha?" I ask. "And you, too, John," I add, awkwardly. John gives me a thumbs-up.

"I'm exhausted," she replies. "I didn't realize how much work it is to listen all day. But I think we're getting somewhere—making some progress. How about you?"

"I guess I'm just doing my best to hang in there," I respond. "I must admit, came pretty close to leaving a couple of times."

"Sweetheart, oh no. Girl, I don't know what I would have done this afternoon if you hadn't been there with me when I lost it in the group."

"Kaneesha, I didn't do anything. Come on."

John jumps in. "The heck you didn't. I was watching you. You were totally there with her. I saw those tears. So real. Kaneesha is my dear friend. Her son was one of my students, and I have her other son in two of my classes. I'm a high school teacher, by the way. You were so caught up with her story that you probably didn't see me crying too."

"Now don't get me going again," Kaneesha says. "I'm calling it a night. Gotta get my beauty rest for the adventure tomorrow." She gives each of us a big hug.

John and I chat for a while as the group dwindles. I can see how he almost became a priest. He is kind, thoughtful, and attentive. I like him. By the end of the evening, I feel that if I decided to leave, I would be missed by at least two people.

Day Two

As I enter the meeting room the next morning, I notice that the circle is starting to seem familiar, in sharp contrast to my impression the previous morning. Paul and Janet enter and, as before, sit across from each other.

"I'm Paul, and welcome back. Janet and I had a chance to reflect on what took place yesterday in the circle, and we have a couple of comments to offer. As we begin our work today, we want to remind the group that our sole purpose is to build a sense of community with the people in this room. As we progress, pay close attention as people speak to what draws you in and make you feel a deeper sense of community and what seems to pull you away from feeling connected. We would also like to remind the group of the guideline, 'speak when you are moved to speak, and don't speak when you are not moved to speak.' And finally, if you had a dream last night that you remember, please consider sharing it, as it may be a group dream. I'll call us into silence and let you know when three minutes is up."

It seems like longer than three minutes of silence. During the quiet, I think about my reactions to Pam and her criticism. To Harvey's pompousness. To Edward's attempt to instruct and organize the group. But paradoxically, in the end, I felt connected to them as soon as they gave me more insight into what makes them tick. I feel less judgmental and more accepting. Was this a sense of community? I still feel a bit angry and resentful toward Pam, and I am getting tired of her tendency to pop off in reaction to what people say. But she often says what I am thinking. I ponder if there is a difference between reacting and being moved to speak.

"Okay, that's three minutes," Paul announced.

Silence.

"My name is Christine, and I had a dream. I'm not sure if it was a group dream, but it won't leave me, so I guess I am moved to share it with the group. In the dream, I am led to some old barns at the far side of a grassy meadow. I'm not sure who or what is drawing me to the barns, but I know I am supposed to go inside and find something. The barns are very worn, and parts of the sides and roof are damaged and falling apart. I am aware of a musty odor.

"I push open the door to the first barn and look inside, not sure what I'll find. I feel a little frightened. Once my eyes adjust, I see a sea of antique objects: furniture, paintings, boxes, old machinery, some covered with cloths, others just with dust. I make my way through the maze of objects toward a large cardboard box. It's taped shut with many layers of duct tape or masking tape. The word 'COHEN' is printed boldly on the top and all sides of the box ..."

"Ralph, here. Come on, Christine. Wrap it up. Land the plane." Ralph moves his open hand across his throat like a knife.

Christine turns to Ralph and stares intently for about a minute, regaining her composure.

"I'm Christine, and I will continue. I open the box. Inside, there is a very old oil lamp, like the ones that genies live in. I carefully wrap it up in one of the cloths and find my way back out of the dark to the barn door. Just as I step out into the light, I wake up. That's it."

Silence. Again.

"My name is Melinda. Ralph, what is wrong with you? Why can't you give the poor girl a chance to tell her dream? You are so impatient."

I'm a bit shocked—first by Ralph's interruption, then by Melinda's response.

"Shut up, Melinda. You dragged me to this cluster fuck, and I've had enough. I'm out of here." Ralph stands up, grabs a box of tissues, and tosses it into the center of the circle. "Here's some Kleenex for the rest of you wimps." He stomps across the room, shoves open the door, and slams the door behind him.

For the first time during the weekend, I feel very afraid. No one speaks for what seems like a long time, but I am not too sure as I am losing my usual good sense of time.

"Melinda here." She stands up, walks to the center of the circle, and pulls several tissues forcefully from the tissue box. As she returns to her seat, she begins sobbing. I cannot remember ever hearing such sounds coming from a person. Deep. Guttural. Finally, the sobbing subsides, and she looks up.

"Believe it or not, once upon a time, Ralph and I were a happy couple. At least that's what I told myself. Some while back, I realized there was something wrong, so I went into therapy. From that experience, I saw how broken our relationship was, so I eventually convinced him to go to couple's therapy, but he stormed out of the second session—just like he did a few minutes ago. My therapist recommended that I read Dr. Peck's *The Road Less Traveled*, which helped me a lot. Then I read his book on community building, so I got the idea that this workshop might help.

"But I was wrong to think that it could fix him or fix us. I am so sorry." Melinda started crying again, this time softly. "But I'm not going anywhere. For once, I'm not going to chase after him or plead with him. I am not sure what I have to face when I go home, but through this experience, I believe I have the courage to let go and make some much-needed changes in my life. Christine, that wasn't really directed at you, but at me. Every time I have tried to find my own voice and express myself, it's 'Okay, Melinda, wrap it up.' But this time, when I heard him say the exact same thing to you, right along with the knife gesture, I saw it in a new light. I am sorry that it was at your expense."

Christine, sitting a couple of seats away from Melinda, reaches out and squeezes her hand.

"I'm Wanda. Melinda, you must leave him. He's abusive."

"Absolutely. Oh, sorry. I'm Victor. You deserve better."

I am about to chime in when I see Janet shrugging her shoulders and Paul responding by shaking his head, clearly indicating no to whatever question she had posed to him via gestures. *Wow, we really need them to do something. We need some guidance here.*

"My name is Arlene. I'm feeling uncomfortable about the direction we're moving in. I'm still back with Melinda and imagining how difficult it must be for her at this moment. I think we are in danger of having what just happened with Ralph divert us from our task of building community with each other. Melinda, my heart goes out to you. I feel your pain and grief. And I am glad that you decided to stay here with us."

Out of the corner of my eye, I catch Paul nodding to Janet. I wonder what just happened.

More silence.

"My name is Stephen. I was moved to speak right after Christine shared her dream earlier this morning, but we got off into another tract there for a while, so I lost the feeling, but now it's back. When Christine shared her dream, she said that she wasn't sure if it was a group dream. I'm here to tell you that I think the dream was meant for me. As I've been sitting here seeing how many old beliefs and judgments I've got packed away inside this old musty barn, I'm seeing that it's time for me to go in there and get rid of all the junk I no longer need; perhaps I never needed it at all. But the one thing I do need but packed away in that old barn was my light. You see, I grew up in Brooklyn. My parents were antique dealers, and we had a summer house in the Catskills, complete with old barns at the end of a meadow, full of more junk than you can imagine. As I listened to your dream, you were describing my life, my childhood, and all that I've hidden away, trying to forget. But you opened that box that was all taped up. With the lamp inside. So to me, your dream was intended for me and is calling me out of my darkness. And here's the best part: My last name is Cohen. I'm blown away. Thank you for sharing that dream."

"I'm still Christine. Among my people, I'm know as a dreamer, like my grandmother before me. My original medicine comes in the form of these dreams and always has, since I was a small child. The dreams come so vividly, and their purpose and meaning is often a mystery, so I am grateful that it was meaningful, and that I was able to play a small part in restoring your light."

No way I could have maintained such equilibrium after an attack like Ralph's. This young woman is pretty amazing.

"Good morning. I'm Catherine. I've been sitting here listening to everyone and have been touched many times. I've also been pretty frustrated from time to time but haven't been moved to speak until now." She stops for a bit and takes a deep breath. "About a week ago, I had a mammogram, and the result came back 'suspicious' for breast cancer. So far, I've been handling it pretty well, but in the last few minutes, I've found myself overcome by such fear about what I might find out next week. I breastfed both my children, and I somehow thought that made me immune. I am really scared." Yumiko dabbed her eyes with a tissue. "That's all for now. I feel a bit better; maybe I can start listening again."

"I'm Emily, and I am bored to death. I'm tired of listening to these long, drawn-out stories about your little lives. I'm sorry, but Catherine,

I don't really want to hear about your pity-party. I thought we are supposed to be here and now with each other, in the present. I am just voicing my displeasure with the process."

Catherine stands up and heads for the exit. Michael calls out to her, "Catherine, don't leave. It's not about you." She stops a few steps from the door and turns to look at Michael, who motions for her to return to the circle. She sits back down.

I am stunned and think, *What was that all about?*

"I'm Janet. It's noon; let's take our lunch break." I realize that I am among the handful of people who have been silent for a day and a half.

As we gather for the final afternoon session, Janet welcomes us back.

"Paul and I want to remind you that we have limited time to build community; this afternoon is the last session we will have together. Both yesterday and today, the group seems to be learning about emptying, and emptiness is the gateway to a sense of community. Our sense is there may still be some barriers to communication and community that are holding the group back from an even deeper sense of community. So we invite you to reflect on what else you might need to empty to be fully present with the people in our circle. I'll call us into silence, but let us break the silence when someone is moved to speak."

This time, the silence doesn't last very long.

"Hello, everyone. My name is Mu-Gil." He clears his throat. "I have sat here and listened to each of you for these days together. When I sat down in this seat yesterday morning, you were strangers to me. I did not know you. I did not care about you. I was afraid to speak to many of you, even during our breaks, because my English is not so good. But one by one, story by story, I have come to learn about your lives and your worries, about some of the very bad things that have happened to you. I am proud of being a thinking man. My culture has taught be to be strong and tough. But I am here to tell you that over these two days, the hard shell around my heart is now cracked open. Yes, cracked wide open, and I can feel again, or even perhaps for the first time. I have come to know you. I now care about you. This is not the way I am used to talking, but I have this feeling that in some strange way, I have fallen in love with all of you. For this experience, for each of you, I thank you."

As Mu-Gil speaks, I realize that he is speaking for me. I, too, find myself caring deeply about these strangers. I feel closer to the people sitting in the circle than some of my friends. As I recall that I had come close to bailing on the group, something stirs in me. I remember what Paul said about barriers and going deeper. For a while, I stop listening so closely to what people are sharing as I try to discern what I need to empty. Then quite unexpectedly, my heart starts to beat faster. Words are beginning to form; I am not sure what I am going to say, but I know something is going to come out of me. I look up, notice that there is a moment of silence, and take the plunge.

"My name is Marie, and this is the first time I have been moved to speak. But I won't be at peace with myself or the group if I am not honest with you. Actually, honest with myself. Since we arrived yesterday, I have sat in judgment of most of you in this circle, for one reason or another. I have been really critical of the facilitators because I felt they weren't doing anything to lead the group. To be honest, I thought about leaving all day yesterday—at least until the late afternoon. I just couldn't understand what was going on, and I pride myself in knowing what is going on in groups as a consultant and facilitator by profession. But this community building process has pulled the rug out from under me, and that is a good thing. I was afraid to jump in for fear that I would do it wrong and get jumped on by the group. So I am giving up always having to be right. So many times, during these days, my instincts and responses were simply off target. Then someone would say something so insightful and wise, and the group would shift. These two days have humbled me as I've had to accept that there is so much that I don't know, and so much that I have to learn. And I have even more to unlearn. By each of you being willing to put yourself out there, I am starting to see how my judgments of others are such barriers to feeling connected; it's one of the ways I have learned to protect myself. And for our facilitators, I was wrong to second-guess how you have guided this process. Your gentle ways allow us to do the work ourselves, without coercion, control, or manipulation. You simply got out of the way and pointed us to emptying. I am feeling really exposed in this moment, but I am glad that I have a little bit better idea of being moved to speak. Thank you for listening."

Much to my surprise, as I look around the room, more than a few people are weeping. I feel like a weight is lifted. As I gaze at my fellow community builders, I feel at home and at peace with the world.

Other people admit to the judgments they held towards each other. Several people make apologies for being insensitive, including Emily, who expresses remorse about her pity-party comment to Catherine. As it turns out, she was recently diagnosed with breast cancer herself and is undergoing chemo. "It just hit too close to home. I'm frightened, too, and I'm feeling pretty sorry for myself. You see, I'm the one having the pity-party. I hope you will forgive me."

This somehow seems to make room for a shared sense of acceptance, even delight in each other's company. We can talk about anything and everything in a real way, and people have stopped offering advice or criticism. There are tears and lots of laughter. Above all, no one tries to control anything, and the group moves its attention gracefully from one person to the next as they are moved to speak.

As the sharing continues, I seem to sense who will be the next person moved to speak. I begin to see beyond appearances and marvel at what comes forth, as if each expression—raw and real—begins to form an amazing, eclectic mosaic of human experiences, both painful and delightful, grief-filled and funny, honest and open. One after another people in the group begin to open, drop their masks, and share about a whole range of personal stories, from the grief of a brother's suicide, to being rejected by peers, to surviving cancer. The room seems to grow smaller. And brighter.

As we approach the end of our community building experience, we enter a period of closure. People express gratitude and sadness that the time is over. It feels like an invisible blanket of peace and comfort is draped around the entire group. We sit for a while in silent stillness, basking in the blissful feeling.

"My name is Phillip." He bends over and takes off his sandals, one at a time. "I just want you to know that I am taking off my shoes, because this is holy ground."

Spontaneously, each person in the circle follows suit. One thing is abundantly clear: I will never be the same.

Just as we are about to leave, Kaneesha begins singing softly. In an instant, her sole voice becomes a chorus:

> *Amazing grace*
> *How sweet the sound*
> *That saved a wretch like me.*
> *I once was lost, but now I'm found*
> *Was blind, but now I see.*
> *'Twas grace that taught my heart to fear*
> *And grace my fears relieved.*
> *How precious did that grace appear*
> *The hour I first believed.*
> *My chains are gone*
> *I've been set free.*

PART 2
BUILDING TRUE COMMUNITY

I would not give a fig for the simplicity on this side of complexity, but I would give my life for the simplicity on the other side of complexity.
—Oliver Wendell Holmes

A night full of talking that hurts.
My worst held back secrets.
Everything has to do with loving and not loving.
This night will pass.
Then, we have work to do.
—Jelaluddin Rumi

Always in the big woods when you leave familiar ground and step off alone into a new place there will be, along with the feelings of curiosity and excitement, a little nagging of dread. It is the ancient fear of the Unknown, and it is your first bond with the wilderness you are going into.

—Wendell Berry

The Community Building Model

Community by Crisis

We've had our fair share of crises in recent times. Beginning with the shock of airplanes crashing into the World Trade Center towers, several devastating hurricanes—Katrina, Harvey, Irma, and Maria—various tsunamis and earthquakes around the world, mass shootings, and the coronavirus pandemic, the phenomenon of community by crisis is becoming all too familiar. At times of disaster, human beings tend to pull together, express their caring for others, and drop the barriers that keep people separate and isolated. Instead of being a sign of weakness, tears seem to be an acceptable expression of the grief and pain of the moment. Spontaneous acts of kindness and generosity abound. Strangers become friends instantaneously. Time seems to distort. People demonstrate extraordinary generosity.

But why does it take a disaster or tragedy to bring out our best selves? When the acute phase of the crisis passes, people crawl back to how they were, staying within the boundaries of comfort zones, relating to people who are like them, continuing their sense of isolation, and relying on their individualism. What is it about a crisis that causes people to change their ways? The feelings of compassion and generosity, and the willingness to extend ourselves, must be intrinsic, since these traits emerge instantaneously, without much of a learning curve. Perhaps it is because at such times, we are most in touch with our fundamental humanness, including our frailty. The intensity of a crisis melts away the masks we wear to hide and protect our vulnerability. Those same masks keep the best of our humanity withheld from others as well. When the intensity and uncertainty of a crisis rattle our foundation, we shift to a different reality. In that reality, we are in it together, and for a little while, our differences don't matter, the need to dominate disappears, and the heart opens.

We have come to know this way of being as a sense of community. Like the oak tree within the acorn, community is already present, at least in potential form. What the group must discover is how to realize the connectedness that allows the desire for community to take root and be revealed. It is hard to trust a process that appears to have no clear path or tasks to perform. It takes a leap of faith.

Community by Design

M. Scott Peck introduced the idea of "community by design" in *The Different Drum*, which described the model he developed to allow people to learn by experience how to create and sustain the sense of community that emerges at times of crisis. Since 1984, the Foundation for Community Encouragement (FCE), the educational foundation he and eleven others founded to spread the practice of community building, has continued to conduct workshops, train facilitators, and transfer the principles and practices to organizations, institutions, churches, businesses, and even families. Unlike many organizations founded by a celebrity, FCE was designed to be independent of its founder and has continued to operate continuously since its founding nearly thirty years ago. Dr. Peck died in September 2005, but the work of community building continues.

Purpose

The purpose of a community building experience is for participants to feel a sense of community with the individuals in the group. Conventional wisdom suggests that the ideal group size is twelve to fifteen. In the community building model, groups typically can include up to sixty people. As one enters a community building circle, the sheer size of the group is shocking. How is it possible to be in a group this large and achieve a sense of community? It seems impossible. Yet years of experience has demonstrated over and over that the simple design of sitting in a circle and following a few guidelines can result in a powerful, deeply moving, and life-transforming experience over a period of two days.

Facilitators

The community building process requires two trained facilitators who manage the experience together. If possible, the facilitation team consists of a man and a woman; it is also helpful if the facilitators reflect the diversity within the group. For the facilitators, the process begins prior to the workshop with community building in a very small group of two people. The essential state of emptiness is necessary for the possibility of a sense of community, so the seeds are planted in the relationship between facilitators. In the period before the workshop begins, facilitators spend time together. Their primary task: to be empty and to have a sense of community with each other. During this pre-workshop period, the facilitators build a strong connection by sharing about their interior and exterior lives. The process focuses on bringing any potential barriers to light.

There is no set way to accomplish this preparatory work, and for each pair, the process will be different. In my experience, if I am facilitating with someone I do not know, we must spend more time getting to know and trust each other. I need to be self-aware and do my best to let go of any preoccupations or worries I am bringing with me as a facilitator. We share any sensitivities that may arise during the workshop and create emotional triggers. As an example, during the periods following the death of my parents, I was still grieving, so I knew that the topic of death might be difficult for me. Facilitators are also human beings, which is one of the reasons for having two facilitators. In some cases, if a third person is serving as an intern and learning the facilitation role, the group may consist of three people. The next chapter includes a more extensive explanation of the facilitation role and competencies.

At the beginning of the workshop, facilitators introduce themselves briefly, review the FCE founding dream and mission statement, explain the guidelines, read the story "The Rabbi's Gift," and call the group in and out of three minutes of silence.

Guidelines

The community building model itself is paradoxical in that it establishes a structure without much structure. The process begins with a simple set of guidelines—not rules—that provide pointers to the path to creating a sense of authentic community among a group of people. At the outset of a workshop, the facilitators briefly review the guidelines, providing a few examples and some elaboration. I have seen some facilitators only read the guidelines; other facilitators, including myself, give some explanation, including examples. Guidelines build self-awareness and ultimately lead to group consciousness.

The guidelines are as follows, with additional comments in brackets:

- Wear name tags.
- Say your name before you speak. [This guideline helps the group get to know each other's names and helps me claim, or own, what I say.]

- Be on time for each session. [We have a limited amount of time to build community in the circle, so please be punctual.]
- Speak personally, using "I" statements. [This guideline recommends that a sense of community is facilitated by avoiding generalizations that speak for others, such as "We are feeling lost" or "Everyone knows that …" Speak only for yourself, without making assumptions about what other people might be feeling or thinking. For example, "I am feeling really nervous right now."]
- Be emotionally present [to yourself and to each person in the room].
- Be inclusive. [Exclusivity is the enemy of community. There are two forms of exclusivity—excluding the other person and excluding yourself.]
- Participation can be verbal or nonverbal. [There is no requirement to speak.]
- Share responsibility. [No one is more or less responsible for building a sense of community.]
- Hang in for the duration. [There may be difficult periods during the process, but try to stay the course. However, if you conclude that you must leave, let the group or at least the facilitators know.]
- Express displeasure in the group. [If you are displeased with the process or what is happening, bring it up in the group, not outside the room.]
- Speak when you are moved to speak, and don't speak when you are not moved to speak.
- Respect confidentiality.

Then facilitators tell the group that each session will begin with a period of silence and that silence may be called throughout the community building process. There will be breaks throughout the workshop at mid-morning, mid-afternoon, lunchtime, and overnight.

Facilitators also mention that they will not be available during the breaks during the day because they will be meeting with each other to discuss the progress of the group. Finally, to begin the process, a story, usually "The Rabbi's Gift," is read. Other stories may be used, but "The Rabbi's Gift" is the standard story.

There is no instruction about how to start or what to do, other than to follow the guidelines. There are no introductions of participants, no ice-breaker activities to stimulate communication, no written agendas with time slots, no group leader, no small group exercises, no presentations, and no hand-raising to be recognized to speak. From the outset of the experience, each person sitting in the circle is faced with the dilemma of discovering what it means to be "moved to speak." Community building begins with the necessity of paying attention to one's own inner experience. Although most of the guidelines are simple and straightforward, in the early stages of the workshop, they are just words and, in many ways, lost on the group. For example, the guideline "be present" sounds simple, but it is quite difficult to be completely attentive to oneself and others for sustained periods of listening. Invariably, when I begin the community building process with a group, I am full of distractions and many matters competing for my mental attention. For me to be present, I must find a way to put those aside for the moment, no easy task given the fact that I might be preoccupied with work and family matters.

The symbols below will be used to explain the characteristics of each stage:

Stages of Community

Stage 1: **Pseudo-community**	
Stage 2: **Chaos**	
Stage 3: **Emptiness**	
Stage 4: **Community**	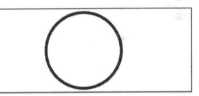

Typically, the apparent lack of structure and organized activity results in nervousness and uneasiness in the group, which is palpable. Sometimes, there is a long period of silence before someone speaks. Sometimes, a person will jump right in, usually making a comment about the story. But when the first person speaks, the collective sigh of relief that someone has broken the silence is almost audible. For an extended period, the group will continue with various perspectives on the story and its meaning or other topics. Some individuals share about themselves and follow the guideline of speaking personally, but once in a while, someone takes issue with what a person has said. If individuals continue speaking about surface matters—playing it safe—the stage of pseudo-community endures. This stage, like all the others, is necessary and neither good nor bad. It is necessary for individuals to test the waters, begin to build a sense of safety, and try to figure out how to participate. People are polite and do not challenge what others have said. But the pleasant banter is in sharp contrast to the inner stream of thoughts and feelings. If a knob could be turned to broadcast the internal monologue on a loudspeaker, we would hear an altogether different sort of expression.

Pseudo-community

Pseudo-community tends to be boring and somewhat annoying, but no one talks about it. Often, the group will lapse into a pattern of posing questions for the group to answer. Sometimes, the questions are directed to a participant to try to get more information from the speaker. Questions may also be directed to the facilitators or other participants. It would be difficult to go through day-to-day life without questions and answers since this form of exchange is so linked to how we live and learn. We use questions to start conversations, to learn more about each other, to seek out direction, or to engage in social discourse. Whether questions are open-ended or closed, when posed to another person, an answer is expected.

It is possible that a person could be moved to ask a question, but questions are rarely I statements. Rather, questions deter the community building process. Why? Questions, especially those directed to an individual, run counter to the guideline of speaking when moved. With a question comes an implicit demand that I respond. But what if I am not moved to respond? When a group finds itself wrestling with how to handle questions, and a person either does not respond or says they aren't moved to respond, the group begins to experience that the quality and depth of communication is different in community building. It's not about having a group discussion or solving a problem. It's about experiencing a mutual sense of profound acceptance of each person, of heartfelt connections, of the awe that accompanies the glory of seeing strangers blossom and display supreme humanness.

During this stage of community building, I find myself sizing up what each person says and forming some kind of an opinion about the person and whether I like them or not, agree with them or not, or want to pay attention to them or not. I assess whether each person is following the guidelines or not. I feel restless, am a little anxious, and wonder how long this is going to go on. I am not sure if I am moved to speak or not, but I certainly have lots of thoughts running through my mind. I experience little spurts of emotion. Pseudo-community may endure for some time, but usually it ends rather abruptly when an individual disagrees with someone or something that is happening in the group. The collective, unexamined assumption is that everyone is here for the same reason, that we are alike, and that it is important to not rock the boat. The group is orderly and polite.

As pseudo-community prevails, frustration builds. Frustration is often expressed through body language. It becomes harder and harder to follow the guideline of being present when I'm bored to death. Eventually, someone in the group or a simple observation by a facilitator will shift the group out of pseudo-community into the next stage, chaos.

As the group begins to shift from pseudo-community, the premise of the group also changes. In pseudo-community, the operative premise is avoiding differences. Once the group enters chaos, it avoids the task of community building. The shift from pseudo-community to chaos can occur abruptly or gradually, but the way the group is operating changes significantly. The group dynamic shifts when someone challenges or disagrees with what another has said. One participant may point out that another person didn't follow the guidelines. Perhaps someone interrupts another person who is going on and on and oblivious that everyone is tired of listening. Sometimes, an individual expresses anger. In any case, one moment, everyone is being nice, and the next moment, the gloves come off, and the group has entered the second stage. Suddenly, it is abundantly clear that, indeed, there are differences.

For most people, chaos is uncomfortable. For some, it is familiar. In contrast to the self-imposed constraints of pseudo-community, the freedom of chaos produces new material for the group. Since there is so much going on that seems out of control, a simple comment can be heard as a fact by one person, as an opinion by another, and as an affront by a third person. The struggle for control over the chaos prevails by way of a variety of strategies. Whether it is a person lecturing to the group about how to move forward, criticizing others' sharing, or rambling on and on—oblivious to the fact that everyone has stopped listening—it feels like the group is stuck. The chaos seems untamable. When the group is in chaos, I am often feeling like I want to leave as I witness—and may be involved—in conflict.

Chaos in the community building circle is more acute and less subtle. When pseudo-community is broken and someone expresses their dissatisfaction with the process, says they're bored, or takes issue with what someone said, the games begin. The shift can be abrupt and dramatic. Politeness is shattered when a person, in an attempt to follow the guidelines, expresses displeasure in the group and admits, "I'm tired of hearing about that story," or "We aren't getting anywhere in this group," or "I'm getting really pissed off." Then someone else chimes in with "I disagree," or "I'm getting angry, too," and the shift to chaos has occurred. Chaos can erupt on many fronts or focus on a single person or topic. The pace is fast, with people trying to jump in and add their voice. The only people paying attention to the guideline, speak when you are moved to speak and don't speak when you are not moved, are the silent ones who are waiting for signs of becoming moved, but not being quite sure what to look for. Above all, there seems to be no space between voices. At moments, it reminds me of the difficulty of making a left turn against heavy traffic. From the participant's perspective, it appears that the so-called facilitators are just sitting there, doing nothing. How strange and different from most meetings or workshops.

Listening is difficult in pseudo-community, but it is even more difficult during chaos. My own experience of chaos is that people are talking or waiting to talk. The tedium that is characteristic of the first stage is replaced with more energy as the sparks fly. The pace is much faster, with little space after each person speaks. It is hard to track what is going on because the threads seem disconnected. People seem to react quickly to what others say. Although each group's form of chaos is unique, common patterns develop during this stage. A group is solidly in chaos when the individuals in the group focus on other group members. As Dr. Peck noted in *The Different Drum*, most often, there are "well-meaning but misguided attempts to fix, heal or convert others." An individual may become a project by members of the group focusing exclusively on him or her. As a person who tends to avoid conflict, I find myself wanting to withdraw. I don't feel very safe and am wary about saying anything, even when I am moved to speak.

Often, someone will try to organize the group out of chaos: "This group is so large, so why don't we create small groups?" Almost invariably, the attempt fails by one or more person objecting to the suggestion. What seems to be playing out is the opposite of what the guidelines suggest: Disrespect. Judgments. Criticism. Hurt feelings. Rejection. Anger. Some individuals, distressed by what is going on, try to retreat into pseudo-community by bringing up the story again.

The fundamental struggle during chaos is over control and power. Whether it is expressed overtly or more subtly, the underlying assumption behind many comments made during this stage is, "If we only did it *my* way …" Frustration escalates when members of the group try to get others to do something, but suggestions are usually ignored or resisted.

One of the hallmarks of chaos is confusion. Confusion is troubling to people in a community building circle, especially for people who either like to know what is going on or think they know what is going on. What makes confusion so powerful is that it connects individuals with "not knowing" for a little while. "Not knowing" is a precursor for being empty.

In the end, the most fundamental pattern of chaos is expression of various ways to control, which never work to create a sense of community. No amount of preaching, philosophizing, pontificating, ranting, persuading, teaching, organizing, or intellectualizing will convince the members of a community building circle to be in community with each other. In community building, there is no guarantee that the group will experience a sense of community. In many groups, the way out of chaos will be revealed gradually, as individuals shift the attention away from what others are doing—or not doing—and focus on expressing their own barriers to communication and community with the group of people in the circle. In some cases, however, the chaos becomes so complicated and pervasive that it can seem impossible to move beyond it. At such times, a blanket of despair can settle over the group. All seems hopeless. But as the expression goes, the darkest hour is just before the dawn. When the group hits bottom and individuals give up trying to make things happen, the emptying process can begin.

Gradually, a few individuals may begin to speak about their discomfort with the process, share personal pain or grief, express remorse about something they said about someone in the circle earlier in the workshop, or describe being wounded or broken one way or another. Vulnerability and authenticity are revealed. But often, the group as a whole is not yet able to listen and has not yet developed the capacity to hold another person's pain or grief.

In one community event when the group was still knee-deep in chaos, I found myself being moved to speak. My father had died a few weeks previously, and my grief and sorrow felt especially raw. I choked out my words in between tears of sorrow. As I paused to catch my breath, a woman in the group jumped right in, not realizing I wasn't quite finished. "Listen, honey, let me give you some advice. I just lost my uncle, and believe me, you'll get over it. It will get better. Time heals all wounds." In that moment, I didn't need any advice. I just needed to be heard. No one else in the group said anything, the topic shifted away quickly, and I remember feeling that I had been somehow left out on the skinny branches. The group simply didn't know how to be with me in my pain. The woman who tried to help me was more likely helping herself by shutting down my expression. My grief was uncomfortable for her. It took me a while to recover, forgive the woman, and be willing to reconnect with what was happening in the group.

The gateway to community is emptiness. Facilitators are trained to point the way to emptying. The task is to empty oneself of anything that is getting in the way of connecting to each person in the group. In every group, the period of chaos leaves individuals with plenty of things to let go of. Add these to my inner life, which I have kept hidden, sometimes even to myself.

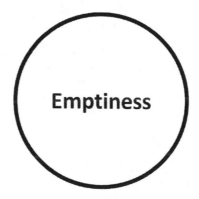

The emptiness stage is distinctly different from either pseudo-community or chaos. Everything seems to slow down. As people become quiet enough to hear the still, small voice within and speak out their truth, listening to others is easy, even when someone is sharing something painful. When emptying happens, different emotions begin to flow. I feel stirred inside, listening to people's stories. I am touched by people's deep sharing and courage. But what do people empty? The short answer is, anything that is a barrier.

During the process of emptying, people let go of everything from preconceptions and expectations about the community building process and the people sitting in the circle to personal hurt, grief, and loss. Ruptures and bruised feelings arising from the period of chaos often come up and are usually reconciled. In my experience, it feels as though parts of me are dying to make room for something new to emerge. As others speak, I reach into myself and find the remnants of old hurts and beliefs, long forgotten but still resident.

On one occasion, I recall the shocking realization of what a people-pleaser I am. As the workshop progressed, I began to witness this deeply embedded structure, and the resulting behavior, to gain acceptance and approval. As a child, I was tall for a girl and often teased by my peers, so I learned to please others as a somewhat successful coping mechanism. In the workshop, as others were sharing, I found myself ready to let go of this need to please others—often at my own expense. My story resonated with several others—a tipping point of sorts—and others were, in turn, able to empty. The group went deeper.

Emptiness is the transformation point. It is worth restating how Dr Peck described the importance of the emptying process in *The Different Drum*:

> *Emptiness* is the hard part. It is also the most crucial stage of community development. It is the bridge between *chaos* and *community*.
>
> As a group moves into emptiness, a few of its members begin to share their own brokenness—their defeats, failures, doubts, fears, inadequacies, and sins. They begin to stop acting as if they "had it all together" as they reflect on those things they need to empty themselves of. ...
>
> The transformation of a group from a collection of individuals into genuine community requires little

deaths in many of those individuals. But it is also a
process of group death, group dying. ... Whether
sudden or gradual ... all the groups in my experience
have eventually succeeded. ... They have all made it
through emptiness, through the time of sacrifice, into
community. This is an extra-ordinary testament to the
human spirit. When its death has been completed, open
and empty, the group enters community. In this final
stage a soft quietness descends. It is a kind of peace. The
room is bathed in peace. Then, quietly, a member begins
to talk about herself. She is being very vulnerable. She is
speaking of the deepest part of herself. The group hangs
on each word. No one realized she was capable of such
eloquence.

The most crucial stage in the community building process is emptying.
I have come to believe that the capacity to empty is one of the least
practiced but most valuable keys to being our best selves and fully
human. Emptying is counterintuitive, in that it is contrary to what
common sense would expect. The word itself has associations with
things to avoid: running out of gas on a remote highway in the dark
of night, adjusting to life in the empty nest when grown children take
flight, emptying the trash, an empty stomach, an empty marriage,
leaving empty-handed, or an empty promise. We rarely examine the
assumption that "more is better." It is true that more is better when
it is a question of more happiness, love, compassion, harmonious
relationships, or well-being. More physical comforts and possessions
can contribute to an easier and more enjoyable life. But a "more is
better" mindset can lead to addictions, hoarding, obesity, and other
health and mental illness issues.

In community building, emptying and emptiness facilitate the passage
into community. Although an occasional community building circle
will have an easy birth and require only a few pushes for the blessed
arrival of community, most groups and people dread, fear, and

resist emptying. Only after a group is solidly experiencing a sense of community following a period of powerful, heartfelt emptying is it apparent that it took a lot of kicking and screaming to enter paradise. Before reaching community, the process and dynamics seem so difficult, confusing, and complex—even impossible. But looking back, the struggle is always worth it. As Oliver Wendell Holmes observed, "I would not give a fig for the simplicity this side of complexity, but I would give my life for the simplicity on the other side of complexity."

When a group has reached community, simplicity and complexity coexist; as differences are embraced, each person's individual journey is honored. The self-imposed collective constraints that are operative in pseudo-community and chaos have been shattered and dissolved through the emptying process. Community occupies a much larger, embracing, and compassionate space in which people feel free to simply be themselves and still be fully accepted, honored, and appreciated.

Without personal emptying, leading to a state of group emptiness, it is highly unlikely that a group will experience true community. Like everything else in community building—and in life—there are degrees of emptiness. Earlier, I referred to community building workshops that rated 2 or 3 in terms of a sense of community and others that were off the charts at 10++. The difference between the 2s and 3s and the 10++s is directly related to the degree to which everyone in the circle was able to empty. In the "kiss on the cheek" workshops, emptying did occur, and there were glimpses of community at times, but there was not a critical mass of emptying sufficient to catapult the group into full-blown, deep, palpable, sustained community as a shared mystical experience. Even in community building where the sense of community is undeniable, some people may not have spoken a single word in the circle. But they have done their fair share of emptying. They honored the guidelines, were emotionally present, and simply were not moved to speak.

What does it mean to empty oneself? Although emptying concludes with a release, letting go, giving up, or abandoning something being held and protected as a barrier to communication and community, getting to that crucial point is a process. The seeds of emptying are planted in pseudo-community and chaos, in addition to life experience that happens before the workshop. Someone says or does something that attracts my attention and awareness. In fact, so much happens so quickly during the beginning stages that there are a great deal of stimuli to sort out. Sometimes, I feel bombarded with thoughts, reactions, emotions, and impulses to react that I don't know where to begin. Mostly, I try to be emotionally present and be aware whether I am moved to speak. After more than thirty years of circle work, being moved is still mysterious and unpredictable. I have learned to recognize my own internal signs of being moved. Even so, sometimes my own reluctance or the traffic jam in the group prevents me temporarily from sharing. I have also come to trust that if I am truly moved, it will resurface later.

When I begin to be aware of something I need to empty, I can only see the tip of the iceberg. As I continue to pay attention, more emerges, and I realize more of what is lodged within me that is ready to be express and released. I know it is my time when I am so consumed by what is stirring inside me that I can no longer pay attention to what is going on in the circle. I may have strong emotions that accompany the words. There may be tears, or not. Invariably, whatever I say is unrehearsed and often a surprise. Even though I am usually afraid to speak, it seems as though I don't have a choice. Finally, I take the leap and begin.

At the heart of community building is the mystery of emptiness. When a group is sufficiently empty, the gift of community may be present. When the presence of community graces the circle, it is unmistakable and palpable. There is a sense of profound gratitude to be in the company of each person in the room. Like the monks in the story, people treat each other with extraordinary respect, effortlessly. Both laughter and tears abound. I feel fully alive and aware of myself and others. The final phrase in FCE's founding dream describes it well: "to make the vision actually manifest in a world which has forgotten the glory of what it means to be human."

Emergence of Community

I cannot recall a group in which I have seen a clear demarcation between emptiness and community. As the people in the group empty and the members of the group can attend to each other naturally, without direction, but out of instinctual knowing how to be together as human beings, community is present and palpable. People I have disagreed with, been critical of, been frustrated by, and, in some cases, wished to banish from the group have miraculously become lovable. I don't believe they have changed that much during the workshop. Rather, my perception has altered, and as Dr. Peck described in *The Different Drum*, in chaos I see people with hard eyes. In community, I see the same people with soft eyes. There are fleeting moments in depths of community that I wonder if this is how God sees human beings: with compassion, love, acceptance, and appreciation of free will. The experience resembles the delight at a child taking its first step or uttering its first intelligible words. It is utterly miraculous.

Stages of Community

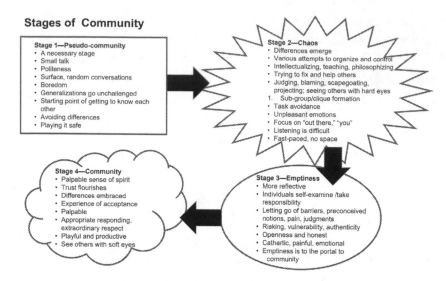

Stage 1—Pseudo-community
- A necessary stage
- Small talk
- Politeness
- Surface, random conversations
- Boredom
- Generalizations go unchallenged
- Starting point of getting to know each other
- Avoiding differences
- Playing it safe

Stage 2—Chaos
- Differences emerge
- Various attempts to organize and control
- Intellectualizing, teaching, philosophizing
- Trying to fix and help others
- Judging, blaming, scapegoating, projecting; seeing others with hard eyes
1. Sub-group/clique formation
- Task avoidance
- Unpleasant emotions
- Focus on "out there," "you"
- Listening is difficult
- Fast-paced, no space

Stage 4—Community
- Palpable sense of spirit
- Trust flourishes
- Differences embraced
- Experience of acceptance
- Palpable
- Appropriate responding, extraordinary respect
- Playful and productive
- See others with soft eyes

Stage 3—Emptiness
- More reflective
- Individuals self-examine /take responsibility
- Letting go of barriers, preconceived notions, pain, judgments
- Risking, vulnerability, authenticity
- Openness and honest
- Cathartic, painful, emotional
- Emptiness is to the portal to community

How to Recognize Stages of Community

Barriers: Patterns and People

Learning to discern patterns within a community building group is an essential part of the community building skill set. Patterns that inhibit movement toward community manifest during pseudo-community and chaos. As individuals and the group becomes self-aware, patterns that create barriers to communication and community begin to dissolve. The free-form nature of the process allows for a broad range of expression as individuals experiment and try to figure out how to do this thing called community building. Every community building experience is unique, but groups invariably use similar approaches to reach the elusive goal of community. Some patterns almost always surface; others occur less frequently. The strategies described below begin with the most common and conclude with those that occur only in some groups.

Attempts to Organize

In the infancy of community building, the need to make something happen emerges rather quickly. Presumably, people are sitting in the circle because they want to experience community, so impatience can surface when community does not happen instantly.

One of the most common responses when groups discover how to build community through trial and error is the attempt to organize. When people first sit in the circle with up to fifty others and are left with only the basic guidelines as instructions and then enter three minutes of silence, most of them are quite uncomfortable. We are so used to having a structure, a plan, a leader to tell us what to do. Stepping on this new ground of community building feels shaky. The uneasiness stems in part from the lack of explicit structure or a clear pathway to follow. How often in life do we sign up to take an adventure into the unknown with so few guide ropes? The natural response to so many unknowns is an attempt to organize and provide structure.

I have seen it all. By habit, someone might suggest that everyone share their name and where they are from as a way of getting to know each other. "Why don't we go around the circle and introduce ourselves?" Sometimes, the large size of the group prompts a participant to suggest a different structure, such as breaking up into small groups or pairs. "I think we should break into smaller groups. This circle is way too big. You know, the ideal group size is twelve." In other instances, organizing the group takes the form of making the room light or darker, or hotter or cooler. "I'd like to turn off the lights. Natural light is so much better. Is that okay with the group?" "I know a great ice-breaker activity." Groan. More attempts to control. No such activity will lead a group into community, although the proposed structure may feel like a temporary lifesaver for those who feel lost in pseudo-community or chaos.

Groups are like babies; no amount of structure, instruction, or direction setting will lead children to crawl or walk until they are ready developmentally. I recall watching my four-month-old granddaughter roll over from lying on her back to her tummy. After umpteen attempts, she finally succeeded—when she was ready and had mastered the maneuvers needed to accomplish her task.

Breaking into smaller groups, turning the lights on or off, or adjusting the temperature won't make the baby roll over any sooner. Nor does organizing the group bring it any closer to community.

Projects

Anyone who has participated in a meeting will recognize the tendency to get stuck and fixated on a topic. In community building, creating a project is one of the ways that a group avoids authentic communication.

Imagine that a group is in its early stages, and people are commenting on the story read at the beginning of the first community building session. The story often becomes a group project; it cannot move from the topic. The group is still solidly in pseudo-community. Typically, a project takes one of two forms: a topic or a person. For example, a woman comments on "The Rabbi's Gift" and takes issue with the exclusion of women, since all the monks were men. Another woman jumps in and agrees, then goes on to explain how pervasive sexism is in the workplace. Several other people weigh in along the same lines. Almost immediately, others in the group sit restlessly, as a nonverbal indication of disinterest or discomfort. A man, Albert, speaks up, angrily. "My name is Albert, and I am sick and tired of all the feminist whining. I thought I'd get away from it at a community building event. But no, here we are. Once again, women being the victim."

Suddenly, the group shifts into full chaos, and it's hard to jump in with a comment in reaction to his statement. The guideline "speak when you are moved to speak" goes out the window or is reinterpreted as "speak when you find yourself reacting or disagreeing." The discussion about sexism continues ad nauseam, and a project becomes the focus of the group.

Or the individuals in the group might take another approach and make Albert a project by challenging him, criticizing him, or questioning his views. Albert becomes the proverbial bone, and the group becomes the dog. A person within the group becomes a group project. The group is moving away from a sense of community, not towards it.

Questioning

It is virtually impossible to hold a conversation without the use of questions. In daily life, asking questions is an essential part of people getting to know each other, day-to-day dialogue, problem-solving, teaching, and learning. How are you? Where are you from? What do you do? How was your weekend? How are you feeling? What do you think is causing the problem? What do you think of the presidential candidates? What events led to World War II? The community building guidelines make a few deliberate adjustments to the norms in place in daily life.

As individuals in the group struggle to figure out how to build community, invariably someone will pose a question to another individual, to the group, or to the facilitators. For example, someone in the group might say to Albert, "Why do you feel so angry about women?" Someone might pose a rhetorical question such as, "Why do we have to focus on such negative things?" or direct a question to the facilitators: "Why aren't either of you providing any direction for the group?"

As soon as people start to respond to questions, community building morphs into a discussion, and the group moves away from a sense of community. Usually, discussions focus on opinions and points of view.

These are awkward moments in a community building workshop because it is considered impolite, at best, to not answer a question. The minute I respond to a question in a community building session,

I abandon the guideline "speak when you are moved to speak." I certainly might feel compelled to answer a question, but it is unlikely that I am "moved."

What I might say in response to a question is, "In another time and place, I would respond to your question, but I don't feel moved to speak in this moment."

When questioning becomes a major pattern, facilitators may choose to make a comment to the group following a break. "One of the patterns we noticed was that members of the group are posing a number of questions. We suggest that you pay attention how questions affect your being moved to speak."

Dialogue and Discussion

In daily life, much of our communications with others stays on the surface. We chat, make conversation, discuss issues, solve problems, and engage in various forms of dialogue every day. Although some forms of dialogue bring us to greater authenticity with others, most types do not. In community building, people rely on what they know how to do until they learn new ways of relating, so most groups experience the effect of dialogue. Quite often, an exchange takes shape between two people in the group. Almost immediately, the rest of the group are observers, excluded—both sure signs of chaos. The two people in dialogue across a circle form a subgroup.

Discussion and dialogue are familiar and comfortable forms of communication, so it is understandable how a group can lapse into this mode.

One of the ways out of being in discussion mode is for individuals to express their displeasure: "I've been sitting here for the last twenty minutes or so, listening as carefully as I can to this discussion, and am having a really hard time feeling connected to what is happening in the group. I just wanted to speak up so I can be present."

Such a statement can make a group more self-aware about the role of dialogue as a barrier to community.

Withholding

Withholding ourselves from others keeps parts of us hidden. In pseudo-community, others see only the tip of the iceberg, so withholding is the norm during that stage of a group or in a relationship. When I withhold parts of myself, it is usually to avoid being judged by others. Because judgment and conditionality are so pervasive in daily life, humans learn early how to hold back as a protective mechanism. Life experience teaches us that we need to protect our authentic self.

In one of the few books written on the community building process, fellow community builders Doug Shadel and Bill Thatcher focus on the human need for acceptance and the many barriers that prevent this basic need from being met in *The Power of Acceptance: Building Meaningful Relationships in a Judgmental World*. The authors elaborate on the ways individuals become estranged from their authentic selves and provide evidence of how the community building process is a liberating experience on the journey to self-acceptance.

During the earlier stages of community building, as individuals struggle with what it means to be moved to speak, quite a bit of internal rehearsing takes place as participants attempt to enter the circle and become seen, heard, and accepted. Withholding can be seen when participants speak about something personal—like putting one's toe in the water, but not jumping in fully. A person shares, then cuts off the more revealing, riskier, or vulnerable parts. "Okay, that's it for now."

Withholding is also connected to the perception of group safety. Individuals may comment on how the "group doesn't feel safe" as a reason for withholding. Withholding oneself may be a conscious or unconscious effort, but the pattern begins to change as soon as individuals speak when they are moved. When individuals are touched deeply by another, the tendency to withhold flies out the window.

Helping

Someone speaks personally from a place of vulnerability and honesty. Several people across the circle are touched by what was said and begin to weep softly. But as the speaker pauses to take a deep breath, another participant jumps in and offers advice. The sense of the moment, the realness, the connections that are being woven with heartstrings are shattered by a well-meaning but misguided attempt to fix and heal. Here is what the "helpful" words are really expressing: "What you are saying is difficult for me to hear, so let me try to make you feel better; let me help you, so that I don't have to feel your pain."

As a person who has worked in the helping professions for thirty-plus years, the first time I realized that many of my attempts to help were self-serving, it was a bitter pill to swallow. The realization shook my very ground of being. I still am a helping person, but my ways of doing so have changed. Most of the help I provide these days is asking open questions that lead individuals and groups to find their own answers. The best help I can give is to listen attentively, without judgment.

Self-Conscious versus Self-Aware

During the community building process, individuals seem to shift from being self-conscious to becoming self-aware. Feeling self-conscious usually involves a sense of discomfort and preoccupation with how one is perceived by others. Although people are experimenting with being moved to speak, trying to use I statements, and being emotionally present, the group does not feel very safe early on. Self-consciousness also involves fear—of being judged, feeling too exposed, doing it wrong, being jumped on, or being embarrassed.

As individuals begin to express themselves in more authentic ways, self-consciousness is transformed into self-awareness. Instead of paying attention to how I am saying something while I'm saying it—which makes me less present and real in the moment—I learn to trust the process, myself, the others in the group, and the gift of people being moved to speak.

Disclosure versus Emptying/Being Moved to Speak

It is common for community builders to have been in some other group, such as a support group or group therapy, so it is easy to see the guidelines as similar. Through participation in different group experiences over the years, I learned all about how to disclose things about myself and my inner life. Perhaps, on occasions, I stumbled into real emptying. But none of these experiences introduced the guideline of being moved to speak.

In most of those other group experiences, the work in the group had a lot to do with being assessed by other members, getting advice, feeling judged, being called on to respond to a question, and having long discussions that went nowhere. In a nutshell, chaos was the foundation.

Each time people in the circle speak, they are disclosing. In early stages, before the need to control oneself and others has dissolved, disclosure tends to be deliberate and measured. For some, speaking at all may seem risky. Disclosure, like pseudo-community and chaos, is a necessary step on the path to discerning what it means to be moved to speak and emptying.

A decision to disclose is still a conscious choice. I'm not so sure that being moved to speak and, in particular, being moved to empty myself are conscious decisions. By paying attention to whether I am moved to speak, I must discern whether something within and beyond me is stirring me, registering within me, calling me to have my voice heard by the group. I don't decide to speak or share what is moving inside me, but rather, surrender to it and all the expression to flow—without rehearsing, controlling, or editing.

Judgments

One single judgmental thought is a small act of violence. If you accept that thoughts are things that can be transmitted, when you look at people with disdain or disgust, they are affected by your thoughts. Likewise, sending positive and loving thoughts to someone can also change that person. Some would call this prayer. If you have ever said a prayer—silently or out loud—some part of you is open to the possibility that thoughts and ideas can affect reality.

Judging others is an inevitable pattern that surfaces in community building, especially during chaos. The guideline "voice displeasure in the group" is often misinterpreted as "speak up about your judgments of others." When I judge another, I make them wrong, bad, less than. To judge is to exclude. Most often, judgments are made based on just part of the story. If I hear the whole story, my judgments soften or disappear. In community building, emptying oneself of judgments is essential. The guideline "be inclusive, avoid exclusivity" provides the guidance.

Do a little exercise. During a day, or for just an hour, write down every instance when you judge another person. It doesn't matter where you are, if people are around. It could even work watching television.

Here's part of my own list from an hour at O'Hare Airport on a Friday afternoon:

- "Can't that mother do something about her screaming toddler?"
- "The airline should have notified us about the delay sooner. I wouldn't have had to sit for an hour in rush hour traffic."
- "No way am I going to sit next to that guy at the gate waiting area." (Of course, he ends up in the seat next to me on the plane.)
- "I don't like that flight attendant. She's got an attitude."

Another exercise: Count how many times you say "should" in a day.

Here's the bad news: You probably have a pretty long list of judgments you generate daily. The good news is that the second you start paying attention and noticing, writing down, or counting the judgmental thoughts, you will begin to realize that making a judgment is a choice.

And now for a third, much more difficult exercise: Divide the page into three columns. In the first column, write down the names of people who are closest to you in your life—family, friends, colleagues.

In the middle column, list the judgments you hold about each person. Then in the third column, list how your judgment has affected your relationship with that person.

Out There versus in Here

All patterns that form during the first two stages of community building are an expression of avoidance of the task to build community. Early on, the issue of safety is a concern for most participants. When others in the group are sharing their opinions about "The Rabbi's Gift," figuring out how to avoid "we" statements and use "I" statements and dodging conflict that erupts during chaos, it is easy to conclude that "this group is not safe." Yet those sitting in the circle are present to learn how to build community.

During pseudo-community and chaos, the underlying and unexamined assumption most participants hold is that others in the group need to make me feel safe. The voice inside my head says, "If others aren't being open, then I won't be either. If someone is going to jump on me after I share, I won't share." I am still attempting to control others through my thoughts. "Why doesn't Cynthia just stop talking? Obviously, she is not moved to speak. She is breaking the rules over and over."

In most groups, the pathway to feeling safe in the group begins with individuals sharing about their personal struggles out there in life. Several people in the group speak about their fathers and their relationships. Suddenly, I am moved to speak about my dad and the sorrow I experienced watching him die slowly from lung cancer— mind and spirit fully intact. The tears he shed that autumn in 2001 were not about his own death, but about leaving my mother, his wife of fifty-two years, to fend for herself. As I share my memories, I let go of some old grief still lurking.

Certainly, groups can experience a sense of community by sharing about personal lives and struggles, but to some degree, the focus on "out there" can be a barrier to deeper community. Authentic sharing and emptying of individual pain moves a group toward community, but when it involves circumstances outside of the community building circle, the risk is lower. Ultimately, as I sit in the circle, I realize that others do not make me feel safe, but it is up to me to risk. I am in charge of my personal sense of safety. It is much riskier to communicate openly about my response to people in the circle.

It is impossible to engage in community building with others without creating feelings, misunderstandings, and conflicts. Avoidance of issues in the here-and-now in the circle must be out in the open for community to emerge. If a group fails to address the issues that develop and erupt between people sitting in the circle, the depth of community will be diminished. During pseudo-community and chaos, in particular, most individuals are silently judging, criticizing, analyzing, and pigeon-holing other. Or perhaps I am deciding who I like and want to connect with and who I want to avoid. All of these thoughts are examples of excluding others.

Until individuals in the group move from the pain experienced in the past outside the room to inside the room and the difficult issues in the present, a degree of avoidance is still operating. When community building is taking place with a group of people who have a history together, for example, an organization, business, or church group, the risk level and stakes are far higher. In these situations, the "out there" issues are also the "in here" issues and must be addressed, or the group will completely stall.

Subgroups and Cliques

Most people have experienced the phenomenon of cliques. Either we are in the clique or outside it, so the foundation of these subgroups is exclusion. The formation of subgroups is a sure sign of a group in chaos. In community building, these subgroups can be obvious or more subtle. Both are counter-community and a barrier to experiencing a sense of community. What purpose do subgroups serve? They are a mechanism for creating safety—safety by agreement. Understandably, subgroups form during the early stages in community building when it can feel as if everything is out of control. If I can align with others around a topic or point of view, I am not hanging out there alone. If a subgroup forms, is vocal, and persists, a group project can emerge.

The group is floundering. Although people are sharing, everyone is becoming restless and frustrated about how the group is going. One at a time, several individuals speak up and express their displeasure, point the finger at the lack of leadership by the facilitators. Twenty minutes later, at least six people have jumped on the bandwagon. A subgroup has formed.

Subgroups can form around an infinite number of topics or issues.

"The group should focus as much on the positive as the negative." "It is clear that some of you people have done this community building before." "My husband and I see it this way …"

What group and individual patterns have in common is a focus on the other, which automatically causes participants, acting as observers, to separate and exclude themselves from the group. All patterns seek to exert some form of overt or covert control over another or the group. Until individuals and the group recognize that the way out of the turmoil is to let go of control, chaos will prevail.

A common experience is the perception of the subgroups of individuals sitting in the circle who have previously experienced community building and those who have not. These differences usually resolve as the process progresses, and differences serve as catalysts rather than barriers.

Emotionality

At the beginning of community building, the facilitators ask members of the group to be willing to hang in for the duration of the process. In the opening of the workshop, they say the group will likely experience painful periods of despair, frustration, or even hopelessness. As the group enters chaos, emotions run high. In early attempts to voice displeasure and use I statements, feelings are bruised. "I think you are one of the most pompous people I've ever met, and I wish you would just be quiet" is technically an I statement, albeit inelegant. And the displeasure is expressed. Before participants become self-aware of the ways they judge and blame others as a clear act of exclusion, I statements will be tainted with words that can be hurtful. Most community building workshops have lots of tears. During these times, it is crucial to stick with the process to pass through these difficulties, for community awaits the group's safe passage.

Emotional expression does not always equate with vulnerability and authenticity. I have participated in many workshops with much emotional expression that did not touch or move me at all. But on other occasions, I have found myself being so moved by another's emotional sharing that my heart melts into a puddle of empathy for someone I hardly know, as I sob along with them spontaneously. So what is the difference? Authenticity and vulnerability, which may or may not be accompanied by emotion.

Emotion alone can pose a barrier and move the group away from community; for some participants, it can be a way of attempting to manipulate the group, either consciously or unconsciously.

Polarization of Head and Heart

During the community building process, what individuals say can be easy to take in or not so easy to absorb. As the process progresses, I find myself connecting with some people and wanting to dismiss others—despite the guideline "be inclusive, avoid exclusivity." This occurs particularly during pseudo-community and chaos. Eventually, someone in the group will comment on others' sharing, indicating a preference for "sharing from the heart." Immediately, those who have said something unaccompanied by emotion or vulnerability are discounted. Unless this perspective is countered in some way, it can quickly become an unspoken group norm—heart is good, and head is bad. I have sat in many a circle and listened intently to community builders who speak authentically without emotions or expressed feelings. I am touched and often moved to tears at their brutal honesty. The false dichotomy of head and heart tends to impede, not advance, progress into a sense of community.

Comparison with Other Group Experiences

Each of us comes to a circle with a lifetime of different experiences, including being a member of one or more groups. Over the last decades, individuals seeking personal growth and healing have had many options, including support groups, group therapy, 12-step programs, Est training, Landmark Forum, team building, co-housing, and more. At times, the experience of sitting in the community building circle can seem like other group processes, so there is a tendency to assume that community building is the same as group A or B. An individual opens and shares a personal story. "Ah ha. I see, this is group therapy." As soon as a connection with a prior experience occurs, limitations and expectations are superimposed on the community building experience.

What distinguishes community building from other groups is the focus on the group as a whole. Apart from team building, the other groups mentioned above utilize the group process as a support structure for the individual. The sole purpose of community building is to experience a sense of community with others in the circle. In group therapy, people work on their issues and receive feedback and support from others in the group. Although community building is therapeutic, it is not therapy.

Team building does focus on the formation of an effective group but typically does so through a series of orchestrated and highly structured activities conducted by a group leader or facilitator. The purpose is to improve the performance of the team rather than to experience a profound sense of connection and acceptance.

Attempts to Control

As people seek to cope with the dilemmas presented by community building, individual communication patterns also emerge. Attempts to fix or help others, give advice, intellectualize, or convert others may be effective communication strategies outside the circle. Inside the circle, such well-meaning but misguided efforts fall flat in community building. Through trial and error, participants learn that help is unwelcome and does not help very much. Advice is ignored or overtly rejected.

At the root of all these communication patterns is the desire to seek agreement, to control others, and to avoid pain. I want others to come around to my point of view, so I lay out the logic of my argument: "See it my way." Someone has just expressed deep sorrow and grief over a loss. I reach out to comfort them by telling them what I did when my father died: "Stop hurting because it makes me hurt."

These attempts to control show up in groups like a cast of characters. Names and faces change, but the patterns are similar. Meet some of the folks that may sit in the circle:

Intellectualizer: "As I see it, the group is going through the stage of storming, which you community builders seem to label 'chaos.' Tuchman defines the stages as forming, storming, norming, and performing. At this rate, it seems unlikely that we will reach the norming or performing stage."

Pollyanna: "I have heard a lot of sad stories this morning. I just wish the group could focus on the joy in our lives. Why can't we build community around happy things instead of pain? So to start the ball rolling, I would like to tell you all about my new granddaughter. Her name is …"

Skeptic/Doubting Thomas: "I've been a student of groups for many years, and this group is entirely too large to become a community in such a short time. We have nothing in common. We have no goals and objectives. And our so-called facilitators are asleep at the switch."

Hostage-taker: "I've been sitting here for almost an entire day and have heard some interesting stories and discussions. There were actually a few moments when I thought we were on the brink of something, then we stepped back away from it. Unless something radical happens in the next hour, I probably won't be coming back tomorrow."

Preacher: "What we have been doing here reminds me of a passage from the Good Book, John 7:4: 'For no one does anything in secret while he himself seeks to be known openly. If You do these things, show Yourself to the world.' We are struggling with our secrets. I would like to invite you to pray with me for our group."

Affirmer: "Julie, I really heard what you just shared. You are very brave; keep up the good work."

Advice Giver/Helper: "Carl, you have shared a number of times about your connection to Native American wisdom. I read a book several years ago I would like to recommend to you. It's called *Seven Arrows* by Hymesthes Storm. I really think you would enjoy it."

Guidelines: Expanded Explanation

Earlier in this chapter, the guidelines were introduced with a bit of explanation. Since the guidelines provide the foundation for the community building model, I come full circle to close out this chapter by providing a deeper look at the guidelines. The guidelines for community building turn out to be darn good guidelines for living.

Use Your Name, Wear Name Tags

Name tags serve a practical purpose, particularly in large circles. Use of name tags is one of the guidelines that is common to many group settings, such as training sessions, conferences, and meetings.

Although wearing name tags is typical in many group settings, stating one's name before speaking strikes participants as a bit odd, at first. Likely, the guideline is borrowed from 12-step programs. Like each of the guidelines, it serves a purpose. Although I have never discussed this guideline with any of my fellow community builders, I guess that the use of names helps to build trust, empathy, and bridges between the other human beings sitting in the circle. Nameless people are less human than individuals with names. It also serves a practical function—making introductions as an integral part of the process. In the review of guidelines, we say that the use of names helps us get to know each other as well as owning what we have to say.

Be on Time for Each Session

Punctuality is a self-discipline; time-management is an important life skill. Some people have a habit of always being early; others are chronically late. In community building, there is a limited amount of time to accomplish the task of becoming a community and experience a sense of community. Being on time is a practical guideline to ensure that sufficient group time is devoted to the task at hand.

On a deeper level, keeping agreements about time is a demonstration of mutual respect. When everyone is on time for the next community building session, there is no opportunity for judgment or criticism of those who are late. When people straggle in after a break, those who showed up on time can feel disrespected, angry, or resentful. The way time is managed by group members can help bring a group together or create divides and fractures. Being on time, in life, makes me more aware of time as a precious resource and helps me avoid the pitfall of feeling like somehow, I am a victim of time, as if time is a somebody. How many times have you said, "I don't have time"? In fact, we have all the time we have. Barring accidents and emergencies, I have more control of time than I care to admit.

Being Emotionally Present

Being emotionally present is easier said than done. Increasingly, we live in a world that values, encourages, and tolerates multitasking. We drive and talk on the phone, juggle multiple tasks and priorities every day, and text at the dinner table or while watching TV. The acceptability of doing more than one thing at the same time has become the norm. The underlying premise of multitasking behaviors is that there is never enough time to accomplish everything that needs to get done, so it is better to skim through many tasks and be efficient than to get bogged down on a single task.

My daughter is particularly aware of emotional presence. I can recall instances when we were talking on the phone, and she would pause and ask, "Mom, are you on the computer?" She always seemed to sense when she did not have my full attention—even over the phone.

What is meant by being emotionally present, and why does it matter? When I am present and focused on the people in front of me in the current moment, my mind stops wandering and chattering. I slow down. As I corral my mind and resist being seduced by distractions, I become more aware of what is taking place in my surroundings and inside my own body. It is easy for me to pinpoint what I am thinking; knowing what I am feeling and how my body is responding is more difficult.

Like being on time, being emotionally present helps minimize misunderstanding. When I am partially listening, I can miss critical details communicated by another person. While visiting my adult son, I am playing a game on my iPad. He asks for the car keys so he can move my car. "Sure. I'll get them." I continue with my game, immediately forgetting my promise to provide the keys. While a trivial example, our lives are filled with the major and minor consequences of inattention.

I realized that being fully present—emotions and all—made me a much better listener. At first, it was difficult to pay attention for long periods, especially when someone was going on and on or drowning in details. I began to realize that just being present was a simple gift I could offer; my willingness to pay attention was independent of the content being expressed by another. Being present pushed away my judgments about what was being said. I am now able to listen and pay attention to anything, for extended periods of time.

Being emotionally present is closely related to mindfulness, a practice borrowed from the discipline of meditation. Mindfulness is the essential human ability to be fully present, bringing our attention to experiences occurring in the present moment, being aware of where we are and what we're doing, and not overly reactive or overwhelmed by what's going on around us. Being emotionally present—practicing mindfulness—requires ongoing practice, like a runner training for a marathon. Over time, each of us can strengthen our capacity to listen deeply and be emotionally present to others and to oneself. Community building has made me a marathon listener.

Speak Personally, Use I Statements

The guidelines suggest that participants speak personally, using I statements. Speaking personally does not necessarily mean talking about one's personal life. It does mean speaking for yourself and not for others. As soon as I started to experiment with I statements, I realized that it was harder than I thought. My natural speech patterns employed far more we statements and you statements than I statements. I remember one of my first workshops when I felt moved to point out to the group that "we weren't following the guidelines." "Including you," another participant quipped.

I first learned of I statements in the early 1970s when I read *Parent Effectiveness Training* and *Leader Effectiveness Training* by Thomas Gordon. Gordon illustrated the stark difference between using you statements and I statements. You statements automatically generate defensiveness; I statements are more easily heard. We statements make assumptions and generalizations; they speak for other people—usually without their agreement or permission.

Since so much of communication involves habitual ways of speaking, the shift to using I statements and speaking only for yourself required some unlearning.

Just open the newspaper to the op-ed section and read an article. Listen to the presidential debates. Few people question the legitimacy of generalizing.

Using we and you statements and generalizing are forms of avoidance. The vaguer I am, the less I must let others know what I am thinking and feeling. I recall a moment in community building when a woman in the group shared about the joy of motherhood: "I have to say that being a mom is so rewarding and joy-filled. Children are such a wonderful gift. They hold our future and our legacy."

Another woman across the room looked directly at the speaker and started to weep. You could hear a pin drop. "My name is Adele. I wish I felt that way. I envy you. For me, being a mother has brought me to my knees. I have experienced far more heartbreak than joy, or maybe it is because my sorrow so overshadows the happy times. I don't know any more. Two years ago, I lost my only son, Chad, to a drug overdose. He struggled with addiction for more years than I can count."

Adele went on to empty grief that she had carried since the death of her son. Her story was real, riveting, and personal. She was not speaking for anyone else. No person in the room seemed to have any trouble being fully present.

I statements facilitate authenticity, specificity, and taking personal responsibility.

Voicing Displeasure

Although some are experts at voicing displeasure, most people are experts at avoiding telling the truth about what they are thinking, what they are feeling, and how they are reacting in group situations. Voicing displeasure is an invitation for transparency, which is essential for authenticity. A premise of community building is that the group has its own answers and needs to do its own work to experience a sense of community. The facilitators cannot do the work for the group or lead the group into community. Like practicing the other skills, participants learn how to express displeasure in a way that provides useful feedback for the group. Voicing displeasure using I statements, coupled with being moved to speak, make the best combination. Consider the following contrasting examples:

A. "This group is really stuck, and it's pissing me off."

B. "I had a lot of trouble paying attention during the last session. I am feeling frustrated and angry at myself for not speaking up sooner. I am so tired of hearing interpretations of the story. I realize that when things aren't going the way I think they should, I withdraw and hide. So I am checking back in."

Voicing displeasure, regardless of the form it takes, can kick the group out of pseudo-community or, at times, shift the group into emptying.

Few dare to be impolite and express boredom or frustration during the first period of community building. Still, when someone finally expresses some form of displeasure about what is going on in the group, it can start the ball rolling. "Finally, someone else said what I'm feeling." The first expression of displeasure moves the group in the direction of being real rather than pretending to put up with what is taking place. Politeness is instantly shattered, and the group experiences a new sense of freedom.

Voicing displeasure builds emotional courage and truth-telling. The capacity to voice displeasure is a critical element of mental health—at the individual or group level—which Dr. Peck defined in *The Road Less Traveled* as "a dedication to reality at all costs."

Hanging In

At the beginning of a workshop, the guideline about "hanging in for the duration" seems easy. After all, that's why I am here—to build community. Why would I want to jump ship in the middle? In the heat of chaos, the rationale and wisdom of the guidelines become evident. When differences emerge and conflicts engage, primitive fight-or-flight responses kick in. My survival programming is to flee, run away, disappear, and avoid the messiness of chaos. By forcing myself to hang in during periods of acute chaos, I began to see that what happens in chaos is grist for the mill. The issues that surface and erupt in the group are our work to face and resolve. Holding and enduring the chaos creates a crucible in which transformation occurs. If the container springs a leak, the ingredients become inert.

The guideline "hanging in" also includes the option of not doing so. At the beginning, the facilitators say, "There are no chains or shackles, so if you feel you must leave, please let the group and the facilitators know." There may be instances in which participants put themselves at psychological risk to stay in a community building session. The guideline "hang in for the duration" is short-term version of marriage vows: for better or worse, in sickness and in health.

Being Moved to Speak

Over the years, the experience of being moved to speak has changed and evolved for me. I remember the first community building workshop I attended; the facilitators reviewed the guidelines and suggested paying attention to whether one is moved to speak. I had no idea what they were talking about, but it sparked my curiosity. Moved? What might that feel like? How will I know? I wondered. It was apparent as the workshop began that others didn't understand the concept either and were blatantly ignoring the guideline and doing their best to ease the tension. I am an extroverted person, so it was a new experience to sit and listen to what others were saying because I was getting no inner signal of any kind to speak up. I found myself listening in different way. Yes, I had thoughts in response to what some individuals said, but it was clear to me that these were just thoughts and that I was not moved. I found it difficult to make sense of the combination of being moved and using I statements. At one point, I thought I might be moved because one of the people in the group really annoyed me, and I wanted to tell them off, which was altogether uncharacteristic of me. Still, I was unsure, so I said nothing and sat with my brewing, unfamiliar anger.

I didn't say a word the entire first day during the workshop, which was a miracle of sorts. I have always been verbal and have something to say. As I sat and listened to others, I became aware of my inner stream of commentary about others in the group—likes and dislikes, a sense of connection, or wanting someone to disappear. The people were saying some of the things that I typically said in such a setting. Did other people judge me the way that I was judging the other participants? The concept had never occurred to me until that moment.

Finally, on the next day, I had my first taste of being moved. Suddenly, my heart started beating very fast, and it seemed to have nothing to do with what was being shared in the group. As I tried to pay attention to what was going on inside me, the group disappeared. At first, there were just sensations, but gradually, I became aware that I was being moved to reflect on always feeling different and being teased by the other kids. It seemed to start when I had my head shaved to treat a case of ringworm when I was five. Being too tall for a girl. A chipped front tooth from slipping on a roller skate when I was nine. Becoming obsessed with the nose that grew off center as a result of falling face-down on the cement floor in the basement. Feeling so ugly. These old fragments seemed to emerge out of nowhere and had little to do with the themes developing in the group. I began to weep.

Finally, I couldn't hold it in anymore, and I began, "My name is Eve, and I am moved to speak." For a few minutes, I shared what I was feeling in the moment; I described how self-conscious I was as a child, how much it had hurt to be teased by the other children, and how deeply rooted feeling ugly seemed to be. As I spoke, everyone seemed to be listening to every word. I felt heard. I noticed a couple of others wiping tears away. Then I was done. Silence. I was able to pay attention again. Then another woman began softly, "I'm Alice, and I always felt different, too, but for a different reason." Alice then spoke about her experience of becoming pregnant in high school in the 1960s, dropping out of school, and giving the child up for adoption. The group hung on her every word. I could feel her sense of sorrow and loss in my body. What a contrast to the kind of communication occurring the previous day. For what seemed like a long period, the sharing and emptying became deeper and increasingly real. Although agonizing, it felt cathartic. People's faces became softer and almost glowing. A sense of community was emerging.

One of the dangers of describing an individual experience is believing that a rapidly beating heart is necessary for being moved, which is not the case. I have had many other experiences of being moved that are different from that first experience. Tears may or may not be part of being moved. For years, I would cry every time I was moved to speak. As time went on, I was able to be moved without sobbing. One of the ways that I know I am moved is when a feeling or thought won't go away. It keeps coming up over and over, until it finally gets my attention. Then I follow it down to the core. I have learned to wait until the impulse is fully formed before letting it out. Sometimes, I am moved by a dream. Once, while in a group in deep community, I felt my heart grow warm, and the sensation spread throughout my entire body. In that moment, I remembered a quote from an eighteenth-century Anglican clergyman. "I felt my heart strangely warmed," he wrote in his journal. So there is not a single or right way to be moved.

In *The Different Drum*, Dr. Peck acknowledged the influence of his exposure to the Society of Friends, also known as the Quakers, who describe the practice of sitting together in silence at meeting as "expectant waiting" and spiritual receptivity. They stress that it is not a time for thinking, but for entering a deep stillness.

Being moved to speak can take many forms. All require discernment. Am I reacting? Is my heart pounding suddenly because my emotions are triggered? Why won't this thought go away?

For me, sometimes being moved is a subtle nudge. Sometimes, there is no question that I am moved. Being moved to speak is for each person to discover and discern. Even after some thirty years of community building, it is still mysterious. The occasions of being moved have certain characteristics in common. First, what I find myself moved to communicate is entirely unpredictable and unplanned. Second, the impulse comes from deep within me and works its way to the surface. Third, invariably, what I say seems intended for me as an act of emptying but also touches and moves others in the group. Fourth, I rarely remember most of what I say. Fifth, the sense of vulnerability is raw.

Participation Can Be Verbal or Nonverbal

In community building, there is no requirement to speak. Of all the guidelines, the acceptance of nonverbal participation is one of the most surprising and unusual. Extroverts and individuals with verbal prowess dominate life. The use of silence at first seems strange and awkward, especially for people who talk a lot. Community building is occurring on many levels. Some aspects of the process are invisible but can be discerned. Without the pressure of speaking, I am free to listen within and determine whether I am moved to speak or not. It is easier to be fully present and witness everything. In one workshop, I was never moved to speak. I learned so much about listening in my silence. I observed and felt nuances acutely and somehow knew who the next person would be to speak.

On occasion, members of the group will call out and exert pressure on participants who have said nothing or very little. "Carl, you haven't said anything yet." Such a request is simply a benign form of the need to control. Individuals will speak up if and when they are ready and moved. If each person is obedient to the "speak only when moved" guideline, silence does not mean nonparticipation.

Be Inclusive; Avoid Exclusivity

Being inclusive is difficult. One of the most prevalent unexamined assumptions we operate on in life is that we are separate from each other. In some sense, we live in a state of being excluded and excluding others. In community building, the opposite is the working assumption. Include others and yourself in your reality. Enter the collective experience.

Being inclusive means being part of the community, not an outside observer. It also means acceptance of the other, the person who is different from you, the person who sees the world from another set of lenses and operates in dissimilar ways. As I have learned to be inclusive and put this state of mind into practice in my life, my world and relationships are wider and deeper. Over time, I have replaced judgment with acceptance, and through this way of being, I am changed by those I meet. I may be changed in small ways. Occasionally, I am altered and become a better person in big ways.

In recent times, I have watched in awe as my two young granddaughters do art with joy and freedom of expression. Wanting that for myself, I have included a bit of them in me and taken up drawing and painting. After years of admiring writers, and not believing that I could be one, I decided to change my belief about myself and include all those authors in me. And here we are; you reading my writing.

What if the reality was that we are not separate but are interconnected? The guideline that invites us to be inclusive is aligned with the discoveries of quantum physics that reveal an underlying unity of relationships. As I build community with others, I empty myself of the illusion of separateness and enter a field of omnipresent, collective consciousness. I will return to this theme in the last chapter.

Confidentiality

One of the features of the community building circle is that it is a safe space in which individuals can empty themselves of burdens and barriers. For most people, being vulnerable is risky. Assurance of confidentiality alone does not create safety, but it is an essential element for building trust and openness.

How does the guideline of respecting confidentiality apply to life? In personal relationships, there are no formal rules or laws regarding confidentiality. Rather, it is matter of moral duty, ethics, and interpersonal trust. When people take me into their confidence and risk sharing something difficult, painful, private, it is my responsibility to honor the trust they have granted me. Harmful gossip originates in either a lie or a betrayal of privacy.

Use of Silence

There may have been a time and place when people believed that "silence is golden," but in the twenty-first century, the expression is considered a relic of a distant, simpler past. Silence is so foreign to most people that in community building, the use of several minutes of silence is uncomfortable and, for some, excruciating. People feel the need to fill the vacuum with something, anything. The anxiety is palpable when no one is speaking. When the community building guidelines are introduced by the facilitators, they mention that silence will be used from time to time. Another guideline—surprising to most people—is that "participation can be verbal or nonverbal—there is no requirement to speak." At first blush, this guideline appears counterintuitive and seems to work against the intention to experience a sense of community with each person in the circle. So why is silence so important in the community building process?

First, silence slows everything down. People walk into a community building experience or wake up in daily life full of busy-ness. Things to do. Places to go. People to see. Most of our lives are so filled with doing that little time is left for being. The world places value on doing far more than being, so it is no wonder that most us do not have a healthy balance of the two modes.

For many years, I taught a graduate course, "Conflict, Facilitation and Communication" at a Jesuit college. In the heat of conflict, everything escalates. Talking morphs into yelling, then sometimes physical violence. The simple guidance for de-escalating conflict is to follow a three-stop process: 1) slow down, 2) cool down, and 3) engage constructively. To slow down completely is to stop. Stop talking. Stop yelling. Just be silent.

Conflict escalation is not inevitable but a choice that each party involved makes in the moment. Being silent, even for a moment, allows people to cool down. The community building experience is one of the best laboratories I know of for people to learn how to slow down, cool down, and then engage constructively.

Silence is also the portal to our inner world. It is difficult for me to be present—especially emotionally present—when I am talking about arbitrary topics or speaking to break the silence because I am uncomfortable. When I talk, I am exercising some control over the situation by filling that void. When I am still, present, and silent, I begin to make sense of the guideline "speak when you are moved; don't speak when you are not moved to speak."

Silence and being moved to speak go hand in hand.

Being silent allows me to connect with myself and what is going on inside me, which is slow and gradual, at least for me. Other people may be able to snap their fingers and connect with their deepest inner self, but it takes me some time and strong intention. By the way, this is one of the many skills and abilities that can only be learned through experience. As I sink into my own silence, I can listen more fully and deeply to what others are expressing. Others' words and perspectives may cause something to stir in me.

Go in search of your people:
Love Them;
Learn from Them;
Plan with Them;
Serve Them.

Begin with what They have;
Build on what They know.
But of the best leaders
when their task is accomplished,
their work is done,
The people all remark:
"We have done it ourselves."

—Lao Tzu

Community Building Facilitation

Group Facilitation

When I was first exposed to facilitation in the late 1960s, it was a rare phenomenon. Over the last several decades, organizations and businesses have used facilitators for planning, team building, problem-solving, product or project development, and other purposes. British comedian John Cleese (of Monty Python fame) produced a hilarious video entitled *Meetings, Bloody Meetings* that satirized most everything that could go wrong in a meeting. It is still relevant and funny, so check it out on YouTube. In the 1980s, the business community began to focus on the productivity of meetings. During the same period, the concepts of total quality improvement, continuous quality improvement, and quality circles hit the manufacturing world, largely through the successful work of Dr. Charles Deming in Japan. Concurrently, many books on productive meetings were published, and the use of group facilitators moved from the margins to the mainstream.

In the workplace, meetings, retreats, and team-building activities often engage an outside facilitator to orchestrate the group activities, keep the group on track, and manage the time. With an independent and neutral person managing the group process, all individuals in the group can participate. This form of facilitation provides a great deal of structure for the group, so the process supports the accomplishment of whatever task the group is performing. Facilitators play a visible and active role in moving the group along. A facilitator steps into a leadership role when needed, then backs off and becomes relatively invisible as the group does its work.

Group facilitation is a technique that many people have experienced. Although a group leader or manager may use participative approaches in running a meeting or work session, the leader remains in charge and controls the agenda. The focus typically is on the task at hand—seeking or sharing information, discussing an issue or idea, or solving a problem. When a task requires more time and attention, an extended meeting may take place to plan a project, reach consensus on an issue or policy, or do team building. The use of a facilitator also allows the leader to participate fully in the group process rather than manage it.

As a facilitator of a group process, my role is to be a neutral party, establish a level playing field for the participants, and provide guidance and structure for the process so the group can accomplish its task. Guidelines that encourage open and constructive communication are present or developed by the group as a way of establishing some healthy norms. A key part of the facilitation role is guiding the group moving through the agenda, focusing the discussion on the task at hand, and being a timekeeper. Depending on the situation and the group, I provide more or less structure and direction.

The fundamental premise of group facilitation is, the group, not the facilitator, has the answers. The facilitator's job is to ask the right questions and to create conditions that allow participants to discover their own shared solutions. When a group gets bogged down in too many irrelevant details or goes off-track too far (I call it going down the rabbit hole à la *Alice in Wonderland*), I intervene to redirect the group back to the topic or task.

In many cases while facilitating, I also record the information generated by the group on large sheets of paper so that a written group memory is visible. In most settings, the group size is relatively small—from five to twenty or so. Although there are exceptions, most groups use a single facilitator.

Community Building Facilitation

Facilitation of the community building process is distinctly different from any other sort of group facilitation. Many of the principles of community building facilitation are like group facilitation, but there are fundamental variations in community building facilitation. Community building facilitators are neutral parties, provide some guidelines, operate within a set timeframe, and work from the assumption that the group—not the facilitators—has the answers.

Beyond these similarities, the role of community building facilitators is unique in the following ways:

- Community building is facilitated by two people.
- Minimal structure is provided.
- The only set items on the agenda are start and end times, along with flexible times for breaks.
- Facilitators offer no advice, wisdom, direction, praise, or comfort.
- Facilitators seek to lead from emptiness versus knowledge or expertise.
- Facilitators refrain from imposing an agenda, opinions, advice, beliefs, or motives on the group.
- Emotional strength is needed to endure the inevitable attacks on the failure of facilitators to provide leadership for the group.
- Most of the work of facilitators is done on an invisible level by holding the group spiritually.

As a professional who has facilitated more meetings, retreats, events, and other group sessions than I can count, the process of preparing to facilitate community building required a great deal of unlearning. Having spent years as a trainer delivering five-day, experiential workshops on grant proposal writing throughout the country, I had developed a finely honed set of performance skills to keep participants engaged. I knew how to work a room to draw people out. I knew how to intervene quickly to prevent conflict and how to size people up right away. Over time, I learned how to use spontaneous humor effectively to change the tone in a group.

None of these skills were useful in community building. My abilities proved to be impediments to effective community building facilitation. As I learned more about facilitation through experience, mentoring by more experienced facilitators, and training people in community building facilitation for FCE, I began to see that community building is not just group work; it is soul work. When we train people in community building facilitation, to determine a person's readiness to facilitate, discernment centers on a person's capacity to empty and be empty—not on their group facilitation skills.

If it sounds a bit like an absolute, it is also true that no matter how empty I become, there will always be something else to empty. I am, after all, human. Just when I start to feel empty, I am full again. And so it is: full, empty, emptiness, fill up, let go, and on and on. Some years ago, I stumbled onto the writings of Meister Eckhart, a thirteenth-century Christian mystic, who summed it up for me with his observation, "the soul does not grow by addition but by subtraction."

Community building facilitation is both counterintuitive and countercultural. This form of leadership is most akin to Robert Greenleaf's concept "servant leadership," the philosophy of Lao-Tzu, and Level 5 leaders, as described by Jim Collins in *Good to Great*, who "blend a paradoxical mix of extreme personal humility with intense professional will." The attributes of the servant leader include relying on one's inner voice, having empathy, being a healer, being self-aware, being able to listen, thinking beyond day-to-day realities, and embracing the concept of stewardship. Collins' Level 5 leaders can simultaneously hold both the "brutal facts" of the current reality with "faith that they would prevail in the end."

The primary job of community building facilitators is to hold the group as it does its work. Holding is a spiritual action, which may seem like an oxymoron. In contrast to most models of leadership, the leadership provided by facilitators involves minimal direction, much silence, little dialogue with participants, and no control over the group. The primary guidance—leadership—that facilitators are taught to provide is to model being self-aware as a group, to be empty, and to point the group towards emptiness, not into community. In one of my early attempts to explain facilitation to a friend who had not experienced community building, the difficulty of grasping the concept was apparent. "Why, that sounds like all you do is to herd lemmings to jump off the cliff. What kind of facilitation is that?"

In describing the practice of community building facilitation, the best place to start is with some logistical matters before moving on to more advanced guidance on the role.

Pairing of Facilitators

In most cases, the community building model utilizes two facilitators. It is helpful to pair facilitators based on several factors, including experience, gender, race, ethnicity, and age. Although two experienced facilitators can certainly work together, it is preferred to have less experienced facilitators co-facilitate with experienced facilitators when possible rather than pair two novices. Unless the community building group is all women or all men, it is also best to have a man and woman co-facilitate. Diversity of race and ethnicity is preferred.

Pairing a younger person and an older person as facilitators is also helpful.

Achieving a balance can also be achieved by adding a third facilitator. This often occurs when training new facilitators who serve as interns to more experienced co-facilitators.

Building Community in Advance

I have co-facilitated with people I have never met before and with individuals I have known well for years. In both instances, spending sufficient time to be together in an authentic way is equally important. Facilitators know the importance of being empty, so when we get together, emptying begins, and we connect deeply, usually in a few hours. We share about what is going on in our lives outside the circle, including any potential sensitive issues that might trigger an emotional response. For example, during the period ten years ago when I was dealing with breast cancer, it was a potential hot button for me. When co-facilitating, I shared my healing process with my partner, so we both were aware that if the topic of cancer came up in the group, it might be hard for me to stay in the facilitator role. We each need to acknowledge and let go of any preconceived notions or anxieties about working with the community building group. If I facilitate with someone I know, each of us must check for any lingering judgments, hurts, criticisms, or disagreements.

None of this preliminary work is visible to participants. The community building between facilitators plants the seed of community from the beginning. I cannot emphasize the importance of this preliminary step enough. If the facilitators are in pseudo-community or chaos, the journey to community for the group will be much more difficult, if not impossible. When I am empty, I am more likely to receive spiritual insight and guidance that comes from beyond my own experience and knowledge. I do not understand how this occurs.

I recall getting a call early one Sunday morning from a facilitator who was in the midst of community building workshop. He was seeking guidance because the group—and the facilitators—were in crisis. Chaos had prevailed the entire first day, and the facilitators were in chaos with each other and arguing about how to proceed with the second day of the workshop. My first question was, "Did you build community with your co-facilitator before the workshop?" The answer came after a long pause. "Actually, no. We were both working Friday and checked in with each other Friday evening." My guidance was to empty with each other, not to try to figure out any intervention.

Although not a requirement, facilitators often let the broader network of community builders know they are facilitating a workshop so that others will also help support the work energetically from afar.

Since I often deal in group settings professionally, I must let go of all the tried-and-true techniques I might use in other settings. In my professional life, I am hired to provide various consulting services as an expert. As a community building facilitator, "not knowing" and surrendering to the uncertainty of the group reaching community are the focus of my internal work. Nothing other than being empty will be effective. I must accept the humbling reality that my personality, skills, experience, and talents are not relevant as a facilitator. The best I can do is to lead by example and continue to be empty—something that no one in the group can even see. Community building facilitation is the ultimate servant leadership.

Preparedness

In comparison to twenty years ago, emergency preparedness is now standard operating practice for public and private organizations, from schools to Fortune 100 companies. Although the odds of an emergency occurring during a community building experience are low, advance preparation for potential weather, health, or mental health emergencies are highly recommended. Knowing the location of the closest hospital is always a good idea. In advance of an event, become familiar with emergency procedures for the facilities, including locations of exits and safe rooms for extreme weather events. Know the exact address of the facility in the unlikely event of a call to 911.

Preparedness also includes ensuring that the room is set up with enough chairs in a circle to accommodate both participants and facilitators. Boxes of tissues, name tags, markers, and basic refreshments should be available throughout the event. These details are typically handled by the sponsor or host for the workshop; facilitators should make sure that the basic logistics are in place. Large copies of the mission statement and guidelines are also helpful but are not essential.

Part of preparedness involves deciding which facilitator will be responsible for each part of the opening section. Who will open the workshop? Who will guide the review of the mission statement and founding dream? What logistics must be communicated, and who will describe details about restrooms, exits, and so on? Who will review the guidelines? Who will read the story and call the group in and out of three minutes of silence? These decisions should be made after the facilitators have spent time building community. As Dr. Peck wisely advised, "Build community first, task after."

Workshop Startup

The next task of the facilitators is to seat themselves across from each other in the circle. This placement allows them to make eye contact with each other throughout the process. Then facilitators open the community building session by introducing themselves briefly and asking for volunteers to read the mission statement and the founding dream, reviewing the guidelines, describing logistics of the site (e.g., where the restrooms are), saying a bit about the community building process and the role of the facilitators, reading a story, and calling the group in and out of silence.

As the group begins its work, the task of facilitators is to stay out of the way and allow the group to struggle with what to do. The beginning stage is full of traps for facilitators. Someone will ask a question about the process that is directed overtly or covertly to the facilitators. "So what are we supposed to do?" or "Why aren't the leaders giving us any direction?" are examples. Indeed, it is countercultural, in fact, downright impolite, to not respond to a question. From the participants' point of view, it can appear that the facilitators are ignoring the request or deliberately withholding information. From the facilitators' perspective, it takes some self-discipline to operate with a different norm. Most groups play out chaos, in part, by directing criticism at the facilitators for failing to lead the group adequately. The information provided at the beginning, that community is a group of all leaders, still is cryptic to the group. It wants to have structure, direction, a pathway to success. More seeds of community are planted, since all these things must go for a group to be empty.

Breaks

At about the midpoint of the first session, facilitators signal to each other that it is time for a break. The decision is accomplished silently, usually with a combination of eye contact and perhaps a gesture to indicate which facilitator will speak. Depending on what is happening in the group, one facilitator might say, "It's probably a good time for a break," especially if there are still long periods of silence. The group may have already entered chaos, and the action in the group may be hot and heavy, with people piling up on top of each other to get a word in. When there is a pause, the facilitator will step in, saying something like, "Sometimes there is no good time for a break, but we need to take one now."

Early in the workshop, discernment about breaks is often easier than later as the group progresses. Particularly in periods of intense chaos or emptying, facilitators need to exercise acute discernment to find an opening to call a break.

On the surface, it appears that community building facilitators do not do very much. They introduce themselves, review the FCE mission statement and founding dream, go over the guidelines, read a story, and call the group in and out of three minutes of silence. They disappear during the breaks and may offer some brief comments or observations to the group just before the group continues community building.

But below the surface, a great deal is going on with the facilitators. What do facilitators actually do? What are the inner and external skills that facilitators must learn?

What Facilitators Do

It is possible to go through an entire workshop, have the group empty itself fully, and experience the gift of community without the facilitators ever making any comments or observations following breaks. I have participated in and facilitated workshops when the group did all the work. In the end, participants became fully aware and appreciative of the fact that the near invisibility of the facilitators had a great deal to do with achieving the sense of community.

In most experiences, facilitators must take a more active role in offering observations about the process so the group can advance and become more self-aware. To do this effectively, facilitators must be able to recognize and articulate patterns that block movement into community in a descriptive and nonjudgmental way. Paying attention, observing group interactions, and seeing patterns are essential for effective community building facilitation.

As participants move through the process and learn how to follow the guidelines, the facilitators are focused on what is going on in the group. What do facilitators pay attention to? When we train community building facilitators, I try to be like a really good docent at an art museum. What does a docent do? Docents act as bridges between visitors and an exhibition; they are the catalyst for learning in the museum. Docents help visitors see features of a work of art, object or display that might be overlooked. It is the docent who guides visitors on their journeys of discovery, helping them blend what they already know with what they learn on the tour. So as a docent for community building facilitation, I offer some suggestions about what to pay attention to as a facilitator.

As a facilitator, I pay close attention to patterns that emerge. How the group handles the guidelines is one of the first things to track as a facilitator. Assessing some of the guidelines is easier than others. Are participants using their names before they speak? Are people using I statements? When individuals speak, are they being specific and avoiding generalities? Do participants return on time from breaks? Are concerns about the process being expressed? Assessing other guidelines is trickier. Are individuals being emotionally present? Are they being inclusive? Are they genuinely moved to speak? Paying attention to practice of these guidelines makes me rely on my internal discernment rather than direct observation.

As the group evolves and enters chaos in particular, patterns emerge, and like the guidelines, some are observable, while others require discernment.

Observable

- group is fixed on a person or topic.
- members attempt to fix, heal, convert others.
- there is a prolonged ideological exposition.

- alliances and subgroups form.
- individuals withdraw.
- some individuals dominate.
- there is little space between contributions.
- people are easily offended.
- leadership and guidance are ignored or challenged.
- frustration is expressed.
- people attempt to organize the group.
- members project on others.
- they make comparison with other experiences.
- "this isn't it."
- they use language that oppresses, labels, or disrespects others.

Discernible

- listening is difficult
- unpleasant emotions
- judging others
- feeling excluded
- reluctance to risk
- categorizing others
- holding grudges
- polarities: good/bad, right/wrong etc.

Another way of describing what a facilitator does is use the concept of monitoring a dashboard in a vehicle. To navigate, I need to pay attention to various gauges that show how the vehicle is operating. In community building facilitation, I track the stages and see how the group patterns emerge.

The table below summarizes some of the primary features of the various stages and show how to read the gauges that vary along the journey. The features represent the various gauges in the dashboard:

Feature/Gauge	1. Pseudo-Community	2. Chaos	3. Emptiness	4. Community
Communication patterns	Small talk; surface comments; interpretation of story; polite discourse	Fragmented; attempts to organize the group or to fix, heal, help, and convert others; language that labels, disrespects others; lapses into discussions; frequent we/you statements	Personal sharing and stories; I statements; vulnerability; shift toward sharing about what is happening/has happened in the circle	Communication flows easily, cohesively; contributions are acknowledged
Verbal Participation	Reluctant; limited	Increased participation; some dominate; others withdraw; may be group pressure to speak up	Participation more balanced, with new voices; no one dominates	Balanced participation; some people may still not be verbal, but there is no group pressure
Pace/Timing	Varied; disjointed; punctuated with silences	Rapid, little space/time between sharing	Slower pace; space after someone shares	Varied, but flows easily, appropriate sense of timing and responses
Subgroups	May emerge	Apparent; may become major factor	Subgroups dissolve	No subgroups
Topics/Themes	The story; brief self-introductions; expressions of anxiety	Anything and everything, but primarily from events outside the circle; discussion of various "isms": racism, sexism, etc.	Personal stories of pain, loss, regret, self-realization; a return to unresolved themes, events from earlier stages; death and sex often emerge as themes	Wide range of topics, including joy, spirituality, tying up loose ends, going deeper with topics from earlier stages

Humor	Usually falls flat	Sarcastic, at the expense of others	If present at all, directed at oneself	Playful, often hilarious, spontaneous, with no injury
Facilitator guidance and interventions	Only at beginning via introduction and guidelines	Process comments may be offered after breaks; intervention only if group fails to self-observe, self-intervene	Little or no interventions; process comments may encourage going deeper	Facilitators may join group as participants
Risk-taking	Little or no emotional risk-taking	Risking increases, but may backfire with negative consequences	Increases; risking draws people closer and is a catalyst for others; individuals risk being vulnerable, more authentic	Risk-taking continues, with increased emotional courage; group is a safe place
Conflict	Usually absent	Rampant	Conflicts are reconciled	Conflict may erupt, but it is usually resolved quickly and gracefully
Emotional tone/ expression	Anxiety; boredom	Anger, frustration, boredom, despair	Grief, sorrow, regret	Peace, joy, love, bliss, healing
Listening	Difficult	More difficult; people are talking and waiting to talk	Easier; may be painful; often effortless as people speak authentically	Easy and effortless

Perception of group process/ leadership	What is this? Who is in charge?	This isn't it; leadership ignored, resisted, or criticized	I get it; Ah ha, it's up to me/us	Ahhhhh; we're in this together
Judgments	Hidden	Out in the open	Released	Replaced by appreciation, even marvel of others
Airtime	Tentative, usually abbreviated; "That's it for now"	Some periods of prolonged ideological exposition; lack of awareness of impact on group	More balanced; sense of respect	Individuals are self-aware and monitor airtime
all icons from icons8.com				

Facilitator Functions

Beyond the task of paying attention and making discernments about the group, facilitators are also responsible for other functions. Some functions involve "being" and are not visible to others; other functions require some "doing" and require visible action, usually speaking.

Being Functions

- facilitate/lead from emptiness
- co-facilitate with Spirit
- hold the group
- practice the discipline of less is more
- bracketing
- be grateful for participants' interventions

Doing Functions

- maintain nonverbal contact
- manage breaks/huddle with co-facilitator
- provide reminders and process comments
- make interventions
- facilitate transitions
- close the group

Facilitate/Lead from Emptiness

Preparation for community building facilitation is different from other forms of facilitation. There are no PowerPoints to create, agendas to build, or curriculum to study. Facilitators are expected to "facilitate from emptiness." Like any other preparation, emptying requires time and intentional effort. During facilitation, emptying is an ongoing process for facilitators.

Co-Facilitate with Spirit

In the mid-1990s, I was one of four facilitators who worked with Dr. Peck during a conference in New York's Hudson Valley. The theme of the conference was "Community Building as a Spiritual Practice." Over the four days of the event, the group of about ninety people alternated between building community in two groups and meeting together to hear Dr. Peck speak about the spiritual nature of the process. As facilitators, we also co-facilitate with Spirit as each person defines it—God, Higher Power, the Creator, Life Force, and so on. I was raised as a Unitarian Universalist, so my first experiences of the power of prayer and faith in a "Spirit within and beyond" myself came through community building. When introducing the guidelines and describing what we can and cannot tell the group about the process, facilitators mention that there are no guarantees that the group will experience a sense of community, that mystery is involved, and that community is a gift of the Spirit.

Holding the Group

Holding the group is a metaphor, since one or two individuals cannot physically embrace a large group. Holding the group entails listening to everyone and everything without judgment. It means being patient, patient, patient. It also means discerning when to step in and intervene if someone is being harmed and the group fails to act. It means including and accepting each person in the group unconditionally.

One of the ways I hold the group as an example, not an instruction, is to imagine that my energy and consciousness fill every corner of the room. I become a space, not a person with an identity. When I shift my consciousness into this mode, my compassion for others increases and my insight deepens. Holding the group will be different for each facilitator, and it can only be discovered experientially.

Less Is More

The more experience one has with community building, the faster the patterns that impede formation of community become evident. When someone tries to organize the group, fix someone, or complains about the facilitators, it may be difficult to fight the impulse to respond and offer a comment or suggestion. Facilitators are trained to wait, wait, and wait some more before intervening. Almost always, someone in the group will make a comment that addresses the issue, which makes a facilitator comment unnecessary.

After a participant, Abigail, shares for the fourth time in half an hour, Fred speaks up:

"Abigail, I have listened to you speak several times about how same-sex marriage is a sin, and I am finding myself getting really upset and angry. I was raised by two loving fathers, and I cannot accept your judgment of them as being sinful."

Coming from a member of the group, a comment has greater impact and demonstrates to the group how to navigate toward community. Often, when I am on the brink of intervening in a situation, a participant beats me to it. It is a good thing.

As a result of practicing "less is more," I have developed a high tolerance for situations that seem to be out of control. I have learned to trust the process and allow the solution to emerge naturally from the group.

Bracketing

Bracketing, emptying, and being present are companion skills. Since life can be unpredictable, at any given time, I may have stressors and challenges taking place when I facilitate a workshop. If issues are so acute that I know I will be preoccupied during the workshop and cannot be present, I will not facilitate. Facilitating in these circumstances will do a disservice to the group and to my co-facilitator.

Bracketing is another option. When I bracket something, I consciously recognize that I cannot do anything about the situation in the near-term—at least the next thirty-six hours—and I choose to put my worries aside for the time being so I can be fully present. I am not denying the issue or ignoring it; I am just parking it for the moment.

Be Grateful for Participants' Interventions

It is possible to go through an entire workshop, have the group empty itself fully, and experience the gift of community without the facilitators ever making any comments or observations following breaks. I have participated in and facilitated workshops when the group did all the work. In the end, participants became fully aware and appreciative of the fact that the near invisibility of the facilitators had a great deal to do with achieving the sense of community. This is the ideal scenario.

I am always grateful for the ways that participants contribute to facilitating community building. Through experience, group members learn how to communicate about the group process in such a way that changes begin to occur. Each time participants reveal their inner process, the group becomes more self-aware. People learn most powerfully from making mistakes during pseudo-community and chaos. I have watched countless people begin with a we statement, immediately self-correct, and then start over. As people speak personally, it becomes evident that it is much easier to listen to and hear what they are expressing when they speak only for themselves.

Individuals in the group provide examples—of what to do and what not to do—that spark learning for everyone. People learn what works and what does not as the process progresses. Participants learn to resist attempts to organize the group with an exercise, activity, or new group format. All it takes is someone speaking up and saying, "I'm really not comfortable with your suggestion to [hold hands, hug, divide into smaller groups, introduce ourselves]." When a group does go along with a suggestion, the awkwardness is palpable and serves as a topic that may arise hours later, when people feel safer and build emotional courage.

Frequently, the group will self-regulate on the use of I statements or allowing sufficient time after a person has emptied and shared poignantly before jumping in. At times when I have been moved to speak (as a participant) early in the process, I've been vulnerable and was cut off quickly by someone else jumping in; I felt exposed and shocked. I could have used just a bit of time and silence. Almost always, the group will act, and a person will say something like, "Paul, would you mind waiting for just a minute? My attention and heart are still back with Erin and what she shared. I need a bit more time to absorb what I heard and felt."

As individuals learn and demonstrate how to lead by example rather than preach, intellectualize, instruct, or help others catch on. Gradually, the status quo shifts to more meaningful, honest, personal, and detailed communication.

Maintaining Nonverbal Contact

Co-facilitation involves maintaining contact with the co-facilitator as participants continue to build community. It's essential to stay connected primarily through eye contact and other nonverbal signals such as hand signs. Staying connected is sometimes difficult for new facilitators since so much seems to be going on the group. I make sure to scan the group and try to make at least brief eye contact with each person periodically, which allows me to check for signs of distress, dissatisfaction, boredom, tenderness, sadness, or agitation. On occasions, eye contact provides sufficient encouragement to participants who are undecided if they are moved to speak.

Breaks and the Huddle

Breaks take place about midpoint in morning and afternoon sessions, at lunchtime, and at the end of the day. Facilitators use the break time to check in with each other, empty if needed, and decide if any comments about the group will be offered. Although fifteen or twenty minutes may seem like a long time, it flies by, so facilitators must use the time wisely and efficiently. Lunch and evening breaks allow for more prolonged discussion and discernment.

Throughout the community building process, breaks play an important role for both the participants and for the facilitators. Aside from the dealing with the obvious bio needs, breaks offer welcome relief from the unfamiliar kind of communication going on in the group. For a few minutes, people can get back to normal. It is hard to go on a break with people in the circle and not talk about what is happening, so it is the first chance for participants to voice displeasure or frustration with the process, albeit outside the circle. My way of describing our human tendency as I explain the guidelines is to observe that in most groups, more truth is told in the bathrooms on a break than sitting together in the session.

During the break, the facilitators huddle together, apart from the participants, and share their observations about the group. The discussion between facilitators focuses on identifying the behaviors, themes, and patterns that are starting to develop.

Questions to explore during the break include the following:

- How are you doing? Anything you need to say or empty?
- What is going on in the group?
- What patterns and behaviors are observable?
- Are you worried about anyone?
- What comments could be offered?
- What, if anything, will we say to the group, and who will say what?

Typically, the group is still deep in pseudo-community during the first break, so there is still politeness, little expression of any differences, lots of comments, and interpretations of the story. In addition, the break provides the facilitators another time to empty with each other as needed, which is particularly necessary if the group has confronted one or both facilitators or if a hot button topic has surfaced.

Facilitators rarely know 100 percent that a reminder or process comment will be on target. What will be clear is the need to provide some form of guidance to build the capacity of the group to become self-aware and self-observant. Each group experience is different, and facilitators will invariably encounter new situations, so they need to be willing, be prepared to wing it, and trust their instincts. In most cases, the following guidelines will suffice:

1. Wait as long as possible for the group to self-correct or regulate.
2. Less is more.
3. Limit how much is communicated—keep it basic.
4. Identify the dominant pattern or patterns that move the group away from community.
5. When absolutely necessary, be prepared to be direct and blunt, but be prepared for some pushback.

Before returning from the break, facilitators decide whether to provide any reminders or make any process comments at the opening of the next session. Most often, after discussion, the facilitators decide to return to the group and simply offer, "We have no comments to make, and we will begin the next session with three minutes of silence." For those participants who still expect to get some real help from the facilitators, the "no comment" comment may fuel spoken or unspoken dissatisfaction with the group leadership. If individuals in the group repeated generalized or made we statements, without anyone pointing it out, or if a number of people did not say their name before speaking, facilitators may simply remind the group of certain guidelines, without additional commentary.

Facilitators should avoid offering praise to a participant or the group as a whole. Community building requires a necessary and healthy tension, especially in the early stages. Praise may be premature; it may ease the tension and ultimately backfire when the group hits turbulence later. "But the facilitators said we were doing so well. What happened?"

Provide Reminders

Reminders about the guidelines are the most basic guidance that facilitators can provide, but only if deemed absolutely necessary. Suppose facilitators have noticed that in the previous session, many people were using we statements that went unchallenged. A simple reminder for participants to speak personally and use I statements may suffice. As groups become more relaxed and twenty-minute breaks gradually turn into thirty-minute breaks, facilitators may remind the group to be on time. Reminders about the guidelines should not be overused, which can happen when facilitators are less experienced and rely on reinforcing the guidelines, when process comments or direct interventions may be needed.

Process comments and direct interventions require more advanced skills. The uncertainty and ambiguity encountered during community building also applies to discernment about these interventions.

Make Process Comments

In most community building experiences, facilitators take a more active role in offering observations about the process so the group can advance and become more self-aware. To do this effectively, facilitators must be able to recognize the patterns that signal the group is in sustained pseudo-community or chaos and articulate them in a descriptive and nonjudgmental way.

Occasionally, a group will present a challenge seasoned facilitators have never encountered before. Most groups find their way out of pseudo-community quite easily, but on occasion, facilitators may need to stimulate chaos if pseudo-community lasts too long (i.e., more than an hour). A simple process comment like, "The group seems to be very polite," will usually suffice.

Process comments summarize what is taking place in a group that may be barriers to community. These comments are more difficult than reminders and require accurate facilitator discernment and skill in articulating a nonjudgmental observation. Process comments should only be offered when both facilitators concur they are necessary for the group's progress. Largely, facilitators name the patterns that are manifesting in the group. It is also best to limit the number of comments and focus on the most problematic pattern rather than introducing too much information. Members of the group are already wrestling with sorting out a snowball of interactions and responses, so even more information can be overwhelming. Comments are best when clear and succinct. As always, less is more.

Some examples:

> "Michael and I discussed what took place during the last session, and we agreed that the group seems to be having difficulty moving off the topic of injustices and oppression in the workplace. Making a topic or a person a project is one of the characteristics of a group in chaos."

> "We met during the break and observed that whenever someone shared personally and was vulnerable, the group quickly shifted gears and returned to safer waters. We wondered how those who shared might be feeling."

> "We noticed that sometimes during the last session, the group seems to move toward more openness and a stronger sense of connection, and at other times, people seem to pull away. We suggest that you pay attention to your own response to others' communication to help you discern what invites community and what seems to block it."

On occasions, process comments need to be blunt, especially if a group bogs down in pseudo-community or chaos. A simple comment such as

"We met during the break and observed that the group is being very polite" is usually sufficient to invite chaos.

One time, Bill and I were facilitating a large group of about sixty people from an international faith-based organization. It should have been a signal to us that we were in for a rough ride when we first entered the room and one of the boxes of tissues scattered throughout the room had been placed on a stool in the center of the circle. After opening the workshop with all the preliminaries, we read "The Rabbi's Gift" and called the group into three minutes of silence. After fifty-five minutes, no one had spoken. People were writing in their journals, praying (or sleeping), or just shifting uncomfortably in their chairs. It was the longest and most difficult silence I have ever experienced in a community building circle.

Not knowing what else to do, we called a break to confer. We were befuddled. Neither Bill nor I had ever experienced such a prolonged awkward silence—an acute form of pseudo-community. We both had experienced long periods of silence, usually a few minutes, but an entire hour? As facilitators, the guidance we follow is to stimulate chaos if the group remains in pseudo-community for a sustained period. After considerable discussion of options during our break, we elected to jolt the group a bit. When we returned from the break, we offered the following comment: "After this morning's session, we concluded that either you have a very rich inner life, or this is a very resistant group."

Within a minute, the full force of chaos erupted. Apparently, participants had been ordered to attend the workshop, and people were angry about it, which was only the tip of the iceberg. At first glance, it might appear that the group had skipped the stage of pseudo-community. Not so. Rather, it was just very pure form of the stage in which this group avoided differences completely, surfaces were all we could see, and even politeness was subverted. As a side note, the group ended up with a profound experience of community. In that workshop, everything was extreme—extreme pseudo-community, extreme chaos, extreme emptying, and extreme community.

Make Interventions

To intervene is to become involved intentionally in a difficult situation to change it or improve it or prevent it from getting worse. An intervention may be seen as a form of control. In most cases, interventions by facilitators during a community building workshop are gentle, minimal, and focused on establishing individual and group self-awareness. Facilitator interventions should be used sparingly and as a last resort when the participants do not address issues, when there are barriers in the group, or when the group is stuck.

Reminders and process comments that facilitators offer the group after a break are the gentlest type of intervention. Direct interventions by facilitators during the actual community building process in the circle are less frequent but may be necessary, especially during chaos.

In chaos, the pace quickens, and sparks fly. Emotions run high and low, as individuals struggle with how to deal with all this unruliness and conflict. For those who are uncomfortable with conflict, a new level of discomfort sets in. Now the guideline to hang in there during the difficult periods makes more sense. As the group tries, through experimentation, to do the work of community building on their own, some participants may call out others on not following the guidelines. Others might make comments about the process as they experiment with "voicing displeasure in the group." For most people, it is difficult to accept that others in the group do not want their advice, help, reassurance, and knowledge; they reject their attempts to fix them. This is particularly disconcerting for people in the helping professions, whose identity is closely aligned with their competence in giving advice, helping, reassuring, knowing, and fixing. Usually, participants start posing questions to individuals or to the group to answer. More individuals speak, and as differences continue to surface and the complexity of relationships in the circle deepens, group patterns characteristic of chaos emerge. During this period, facilitators pay attention to these patterns and assess how the group handles them.

Although the group can become very contentious on occasion, facilitators do not usually intervene at this point, unless the group fails to act. For example, imagine that people are starting to open and be vulnerable. The person sharing deeply pauses for a breath and another person immediately starts in on a different topic. Most of the group is still back with the first person, trying to absorb what was said. The same, quick shifting of gears happens again several times. If someone in the group does not speak up, facilitators may need to intervene. Without intervention by group members or facilitators, it will not feel safe for others to continue. The group will retreat from emptying and return to more chaos and avoidance.

The next time a participant jumps in too quickly, it may be appropriate for one of the facilitators to gently ask the person to pause and hold their comments for a bit in order to allow some space and for the group to take in what the person has said. When the group gets especially fast-paced with many participant interruptions, a facilitator might call for a moment or two of silence.

Whenever there is a danger of physical harm or violence, facilitators must spring into action. Such instances are extremely rare, but possible. An example of the need for direct intervention is if person gets up and approaches another in anger or with the potential of violence; one or both of the facilitators will stand up and approach the person to de-escalate the confrontation. Facilitators may need to call for a break and deal with participants individually. In extreme cases, when a participant exhibits signs of psychosis or a break with reality, intervention is needed. In both instances, facilitators may need to consider removing a participant from the group.

Facilitate Transitions

As the stages manifest during community building, facilitators may need to help transition from one stage to another with reminders, process comments, and interventions. Some transitions involve shifting in and out of the community building mode, for example managing daytime and evening breaks; others involve transitions between stages of community.

Managing breaks during the two days of community building was addressed earlier. Facilitators also need to prepare participants to transition between the two days. At the end of the first day, facilitators provide a few reminders to the group, beginning with the need to practice self-care. Community building is an intense emotional experience, and facilitators suggest that participants take special care to be gentle with themselves and to pay careful attention if driving home, as one's consciousness may seem a bit altered. Participants are also asked to try to remember and share their dreams, as often people have what may be a group dream that may offer insight for the group.

Ideally, stage transitions occur organically, without any prompting by facilitators. The transition from pseudo-community to chaos usually occurs quite easily. The transition from emptiness to community is effortless and may even seem magical. The transition from chaos to emptying is the most difficult and may require guidance from facilitators.

Sometimes, chaos is sustained for what seems like a very long time. Even an hour of full-blown chaos feels never-ending because it requires so much energy to let it be. It is exhausting. Typically, individuals try to stop or contain it. Mostly, it is a wrestling match with one force attempting to overpower another. Nothing seems to work. Some groups carry chaos over into the second day. A few groups cannot get beyond this stage, although it is rare. Regardless of the number of times I have experienced community building, at this point in the process, I always wonder why I am doing community building at all. This sense of despair and hopelessness seems to accompany chaos, so I have learned to recognize it as confirmation of the stage. However, the worse it gets and the more despairing the tone, the closer the group is to emptying. Sometimes, it takes this high level of frustration for individuals to begin to give up and let go. At this juncture, the facilitator's' most helpful intervention is to suggest that the way out of chaos is through emptying and emptiness.

The wording might be different, or the facilitators may suggest that participants remain in silence during the break. Another possible approach is to ask participants to consider emptying any barriers they may be holding on to that are keeping them from experiencing community with the individuals sitting together in the circle. Barriers are often withheld communications about something that occurred during the time together but seemed too risky to broach. Everyone must identify their own barriers.

For me, when the necessity to empty comes, I stop thinking about what I am going to say and how I am going to say it; it simply comes out however it does. It can be messy, imperfect, unadulterated, and raw. As I listen to others as they are moved to empty, I find myself touched deeply by their courage and honesty. The more present and authentic people are as they share, the more I cry, whether they express emotion or not. My tear ducts seem to be wired to some internal authenticity meter.

Perhaps with gentle prompting from the facilitators or through someone being moved to speak, chaos begins to recede and is replaced with tender vulnerability. When all other avenues are exhausted, people finally speak directly and personally about the struggle and its impact on them. As the first few people share from a deep place of vulnerability and realness, speaking only of their own pain, or realizations, or regrets, or stories, the group may briefly retreat back into chaos, or even pseudo-community, unable to take in what is being expressed. But slowly and surely, the group marches forward, bravely, into and through emptying and emptiness.

As people share, their words and emotions touch some lingering memory or regret or secret. Eventually, a critical mass of people in the group have emptied, and the entire feeling in the room changes. A natural and graceful rhythm replaces the awkwardness of pseudo-community and the disconnectedness of chaos. When others touch and reveal these human frailties and their brokenness, I am compelled to do the same and to peer into long-forgotten crevices in my soul. Inside are memories, of old hurts, of residual grief that cries to finally be released. I may or may not be moved to speak, but I have no choice other than to empty myself at this point. It is cathartic. It is healing. It can be agonizing. It is freeing. How could something that is ultimately so simple seem so difficult?

Years ago, I attended a six-day personal-development course near San Francisco, up in the mountains. About midweek, the day's activities included a high ropes course. The week before, someone had died on the course. I was terrified and certain that I would be the one to die that week. After prolonged instructions on how to tie the knot on our safety belts, I went to at least ten people to have them check my knot to make sure I had tied it correctly. The last event, the zip line, involved a line connected from a cliff to an evergreen four hundred feet below. When my turn came to jump, the line behind me stalled as I desperately tried to bargain with the supervising staff person.

"When you are ready, just lift your legs and let go," he instructed.

"How will I know if I'm ready?" I asked.

He repeated the instruction.

My reply: "I'm not sure I know how to lift my legs."

Again, the instruction. Finally, I ran out of useless questions and proceeded to my certain death. I lifted my legs.

As I was being disconnected from the safety gear, still alive, I experienced one of the most profoundly exhilarating moments of my life. I felt acutely, radically alive. On the other side of my fear and inability to let go of my perceived control, I found a new kind of freedom. "When you are ready, just let go." Good advice.

When the group is solidly in community, facilitators can join in the group and feel free to share and be moved to speak or even empty. Once community is formed, the group has created a strong and safe container to hold all the expression. On rare occasions when a group clearly wants to move out of chaos, but just cannot fathom emptying and one of the facilitators is moved to speak, he or she may be able to lead by example and empty. It is essential that both facilitators are in consensus that the group is ready and that the second facilitator can hold the group while the first empties. In all my years of co-facilitating, I have experienced emptying as a facilitator only twice. In both instances, my sharing was a tipping point for the group.

Close the Group

The final transition that facilitators manage is closure of the workshop. Near the midpoint of the final day of the workshop, facilitators remind the group that the workshop will end; about an hour before the closing, a shift to closure begins. Closure is a period for the group to acknowledge the finality—the death—of this unique community that has formed during the experience. Closure involves a letting go and a complete acceptance of what has happened and an honoring of the transition away from what is finished to what's ahead. There are no different guidelines for closure other than to suggest that the group may decide to honor the ending with a ritual. Facilitators do not suggest any specific ritual.

If a group has experienced a deep sense of community, the closure period may be filled with heartfelt expressions of appreciation, gratitude, and sorrow about the death of the group. If a group has struggled to build a sense of community, emptying, or even chaos may persist into the last part of the workshop. In most instances, even those with difficult passages into community, participants find ways to acknowledge and make peace with what has transpired.

I have experienced many different and spontaneous rituals. Sometimes, a song erupts, and everyone joins in. It might be a group hug or sending a hand-squeeze around the circle. Often, the ritual involves a meaningful symbol that has emerged during the process.

PART 3
APPLICATION

Self-Talk

Rest your phone in your lap,
face down, and look out the window,
the world reeling past, all around, you at the center.

Have that conversation with yourself,
the one you've been meaning to have,
the one where you listen without judgment,
to what you need

the one where you give yourself permission
to step to the edge of the diving board,
look down at the water, feel the fear,
and jump in anyway.

—Keith Byler

Stages of Community in Daily Life

While the focus in this book is on the specifics of the community building process, the experience is the means, not the end. Dr. Peck opens *The Different Drum: Community Making and Peace* with a bold statement: "In and through community lies the salvation of the world." He goes on to say that "perhaps peacemaking should start small" and that "until we learn the basic principles of community in our own individual lives and personal spheres of influence," the reality of global community and international peace cannot be achieved.

Building True Community is intended as a small start by building community from the inside out, starting with yourself, your family, your organizations. By having a better understanding of the community building process and how to go about facilitating such an experience, it is my hope that more people will seek out the experience, see the benefits, and learn how to implement practical changes in thinking and behavior. Even small changes can help to bridge our divides and reduce the fear and violence that result from distrusting the other. The community building experience is a laboratory that allows individuals to practice interpersonal disarmament, mindfulness, gratitude, conflict reconciliation, empathy, and treating others with extraordinary respect.

It is also my hope that this book will prompt a renewed interest in community building experiences. In its heyday, when Dr. Peck lectured around the county with his bestselling books out in the marketplace, the Foundation for Community Encouragement was offering workshops in America and beyond, hosting an annual Community Continuity Conference, providing consulting services with organizations, and training new facilitators. After he stopped lecturing and being the primary marketing force for community, the number of workshops gradually declined. At the time of this writing, a few public workshops are offered in the Chicago area, and several international groups continue offering workshops, but they are few and far between.

In the end, the community building process is most useful when the principles and practices can be applied in daily life. Although community building can be a powerful learning experience for individuals and groups, attending an in-person workshop may not be immediate. Over time, I have come to see daily life through the lens of community building stages. I notice what is going on in each situation or setting. I pay attention to what I am thinking and feeling. I watch for patterns of communication and behavior, and ascertain what stage or mode of being is playing out in a relationship, a family, a group, an organization, or even in society at large.

Although the actual community building experience is the best way to learn the principles and practices, a workshop setting is outside of day-to-day living. The principles and practices that promote a sense of community can be integrated into day-to-day life with or without participation in a community building workshop. A community building experience is a laboratory of sorts. Application after the experience is what makes the difference. New drugs that never make it beyond the laboratory and clinical trials are not much help to anyone.

While the focus in this book is on the specifics of the community building process, the experience is the means, not the end. Dr. Peck opens *The Different Drum: Community Making and Peace* with a bold statement: "In and through community lies the salvation of the world." He goes on to say that "perhaps peacemaking should start small" and that "until we learn the basic principles of community in our own individual lives and personal spheres of influence," the reality of global community and international peace cannot be achieved.

Building True Community is intended as a small start by building community from the inside out, starting with yourself, your family, your organizations. By having a better understanding of the community building process and how to go about facilitating such an experience, it is my hope that more people will seek out the experience, see the benefits, and learn how to implement practical changes in thinking and behavior. Even small changes can help to bridge our divides and reduce the fear and violence that result from distrusting the other. The community building experience is a laboratory that allows individuals to practice interpersonal disarmament, mindfulness, gratitude, conflict reconciliation, empathy, and treating others with extraordinary respect.

Although reading about community building cannot replace the actual experience, most of us have a lifetime of learning from books, so the following two chapters focus on practical steps to get started with community building. Willing and courageous individuals are fully capable of taking the principles and practices into daily life.

In taking community building into our daily lives, a first step can be to recognize how the stages play out in our relationships, families, organizations, communities, and society. Each stage looks different in different contexts. Pseudo-community in a personal relationship looks different than organizational pseudo-community. By reviewing examples of stages in various settings, it becomes easier to shift from being solely a participant in interpersonal dynamics to being able to choose how to respond more consciously. Being able to assess the stage can awaken the observer within, which can facilitate movement in the direction of community.

There is a time and a place for pseudo-community; like all stages, it serves a purpose. Different stages generate different sorts of feelings, so it is natural to view pseudo-community and chaos as less valuable than emptiness or community. Neither good nor bad, they are all needed for the healthy development of a group. Anyone who has raised a child and braved it through the terrible twos or the ups-and-downs of adolescence can predict that their child will mature and grow beyond these developmental stages. Some adults have arrested development and are still prone to toddler tantrums. Some children, referred to as "old souls," are wise and mature beyond their years. Each group has its own unique path through the stages and may stop along the way and not progress. Members of any given group may individually be in a different stage than others in the group.

Pseudo-Community in Relationships and Families

Most have experienced the awkwardness and discomfort of meeting others for the first time or being with a new group of people. Pseudo-community is easy to recognize, as it serves as the baseline for many of our day-to-day encounters. Surface-level communications and small talk in our interactions with others are natural parts of social exchange.

In relationships, the early stages are referred to as the honeymoon phase. All seems to be bliss. Research by experts indicates that the infatuation stage lasts approximately three months before facing daily realties moves to the foreground (the actual time may be more or less, depending on the relationship). Pseudo-community in a relationship may continue for much longer. I met my husband through a mutual friend, and we were engaged ten days later, married within three months, and conceived our first child on the honeymoon. Looking back, our relationship operated in pseudo-community for an extended period before progressing into our version of chaos.

Most of this book was written while on one of my writing cruises to the Caribbean over the last several years, before the coronavirus pandemic. Knowing how easily distracted I can be with work and family pressures, I periodically book a cruise by myself just to write. Well, mostly write. If I were able to eavesdrop on all the conversations going on with the thousands of people on board at any given time, my guess is that at least 80 percent are engaging in small talk. I do my best to avoid conversations during these cruises, but they are inevitable as I sit in my lounge chair or at a dining table. When a conversation does ensue, it usually begins with "Where are you from?" then continues with a polite exchange for a few minutes.

I did not grow up with social media, but Facebook and Twitter are perfect platforms for pseudo-community. Although there are many advantages to social media, there are also growing concerns that the friendships developed through social media leave one frustrated, lonely, and struggling to connect on a deeper, more emotionally meaningful level. There is also a concern that individuals might forgo real-life interactions to maintain online communication.

I recall getting into a taxicab in Manhattan one morning, only to be held captive by the cabdriver's detailed, heart-wrenching story of his most recent troubles with his wife. I was not ready for such intimacy in our first—and last—fifteen minutes of interaction. I would have far preferred to talk weather and the Yankees.

Suggesting that movement toward a greater sense of community is needed does not mean that we stop pseudo-community or chaos. Rather, it means that individuals learn and use the principles and skills to move beyond those stages and to build the capacity to embrace the value of emptying. We need not abandon the important function pseudo-community plays in our relationships with others.

Pseudo-Community in Organizations

Pseudo-community has a stronghold in most groups and organizations. Playing it safe and coloring inside the lines is tantamount to acceptance in most organizational settings. We have all seen what happens to people who rock the boat.

Organizational cultures often admonish mixing personal and professional lives. In a consulting assignment years ago, I worked with Eli, a systems department executive in a large financial services company. Part of my consulting assignment included executive coaching. As I became familiar with Eli and his staff, I learned that several people confessed that they were "afraid" of Eli. This impression was in such contrast to my experience of the man. He was truly a kind, thoughtful, and tender-hearted person. As I explored the reasons for this response, his staff told me that "he won't talk to me." With more probing, it came down to the fact that when he encountered people throughout the day outside of meetings—standing by the elevator or in the cafeteria line—he was silent.

When I shared the feedback with him, his response was simple: "I don't do small talk. Actually, I don't do it well." I explained that his silence was misinterpreted; it created distance and discomfort. We spent a few coaching sessions practicing small talk until he felt more comfortable and competent. Dutifully, he changed his ways and started asking, "How is your day going?" or commenting on the weather or other banalities. Within a few weeks, the buzz around the department was what a "nice guy" he was.

There is a time and a place for pseudo-community, but the depth of relationships is limited.

Pseudo-Community in Society

On a societal level, the practice of diplomacy illustrates how pseudo-community can be codified. Diplomatic protocol calls for tact, good manners, ceremonial rules specific to a given culture, etiquette, and courteousness. Diplomacy aids communication, builds mutual trust, and paves the way for the inevitable differences and contention that exist in international relations. As Sir Isaac Newton once said, "Tact is the art of making a point without making an enemy."

Some years ago, I was invited to Japan to facilitate a community building experience. I was reluctant to go for several reasons. First, the sponsors were not sure how many people would attend. Second, I was concerned that the interpersonal communication norms in Japanese culture, such as saving face, indirect communication, and politeness might preclude movement beyond pseudo-community and be a barrier to community building. Regardless, I booked a flight and went anyway. About twenty people showed up for the event, some traveling from distant islands. Much to my surprise, the group abandoned small talk and niceties almost immediately and moved quickly through chaos. Rarely have I seen a group move so easily into emptying. One after another, individuals spoke of the sadness they carried about having to pretend, about feeling disconnected from others, and about how much they longed for human warmth, connection, and touch.

Chaos in Relationships and Families

Describing the stages in daily life has its pitfalls, as the stages are not always sequential or pure. In relationships, groups, or organizations, day-to-day life is more likely to be a hybrid of pseudo-community and chaos. Pseudo-community in daily life tends to be boring rather than anxiety-provoking. Differences may be out in the open, but emotions may not be triggered, or the attempts to obliterate differences and control others may not have surfaced. Pure chaos is all too familiar.

Shortly after my husband and I first met, we experienced a moment of chaos. Looking back, it was an example of the differences in our two family cultures. I grew up with two scientists, transplanted from Texas to suburban Cincinnati, who were staunch Unitarian Universalists. Tony grew up in an immigrant, Catholic family—from Spain on his mother's side and Croatia on his father's. Their family of six lived in a two-room apartment two blocks from the Hudson River in Greenwich Village.

One evening, we were having dinner at a restaurant the Village. The food arrived, and immediately his fork was in my plate, an intrusion I had never experienced. "How dare he?" was clearly written on my face. We both laughed about it, and the moment passed, but our different perspectives on food became a low-grade issue that surfaced when parenting our children. For example, milk became an issue. He insisted that milk was mucus-forming and should be avoided; I cited scientific evidence of how healthy milk was for growing children. We were both right. This example is trivial but illustrative of how chaos can play out in relationships and the many ways that the need to control can surface.

It is a rare human being who has never experienced being rejected, judged, ostracized, blamed, or hurt by harsh words or actions by someone close to them. Although there may be exceptions, human beings experience the lion's share of chaos in personal and family relationships.

Chaos in families is inevitable and may devolve from periodic episodes to dysfunction as the norm. Dysfunctional families experience conflict, misbehavior, or abuse. In many cases, one parent is abusive and dominant, and the other turns a blind eye to the behavior. Typical behaviors include

- lack of empathy,
- poor communication,

- emotional or physical abuse,
- control,
- excessive criticism,
- drug or alcohol abuse,
- perfectionism,
- denial, and
- disrespect of boundaries.

I grew up in a family largely protected from chaos and dysfunction, but we were not immune. From the list above, our version of chaos involved the fear and unpredictability of my father's anger, which seemed to keep us all walking on eggshells. My dad always seemed to be mad, not really at anyone, but just angry. He would yell at the TV and other drivers on the road. I remember being so frightened in the car one afternoon that I insisted that he stop (on the interstate) and let me out of the car. He stopped raging. My mother's response was always, "Everything is fine. He isn't angry," so I was left with my own experience and fear, alongside my mother's denial. Of course, I assumed that all these behaviors were normal.

Despite the discomfort of chaos in relationships, it is necessary for growth and change. When I welcome and allow myself to be changed or affected by something new and difficult, I grow. When I fear someone different, the walls and barriers begin to build as a means of protection. Tony's fork in my plate changed me. Our meals together became more fun, and I was able to taste more and different foods. In *The Road Less Traveled*, Dr. Peck said there were two reasons for getting married: children and friction.

Chaos in Groups and Organizations

Chaos happens in every group, organization, relationship, or family. It is an inevitable part of the movement of life and growth in relationships and society. As with the first stage, chaos is a difficult but necessary stage because it is through our differences that new possibilities and solutions arise. Diversity and differences are the raw materials for progress.

Most people manage to grow and develop as human beings and learn that it is not always possible to have things go the way they might choose. But when it comes to interacting in a group setting, be it the family, workplace, or community, few people realize how deeply they are affected by the dynamic of chaos. Rather than being able to spot the ways that chaos can manifest, matters get personal. Typically, the assumption of hopelessness is summarized by "It's just personalities," as if nothing can be done to deal with individual differences. In the end, it is not the differences in personalities, but the inability for individuals to handle the attempts for one personality to dominate or control another.

In the absence of recognizing the characteristics of chaos—and knowing the way out—a difference of opinion, a miscommunication, a facial expression, or a judgmental statement can escalate slowly (or quickly) into irreconcilable differences. The only way out is to leave, which seems to be the only way of exerting control. Quitting a job. Getting fired. Filing for divorce. Forcing someone out. Forming a new group. Certainly, there are situations in which an exit is the most prudent action. In most cases, however, there are options other than taking it personally and quitting or being excommunicated. As the conflict develops and evolves, confusion and complexity also multiply, to the point that it seems impossible to sort everything out. Attempts to do so only add to the mess. As the situation continues without resolution, the group or relationship is stuck and falls into the state of chronic chaos. Eventually, the condition of relationships, communications, and behavior seem normal. Also, chaos, like adolescence, is a stage of development. When it is arrested, it is abnormal.

One of the most obvious signs of chronic chaos is when individuals take the issues underground. Rather than expressing a concern out in the open, I share my frustration with a friend who is not involved in the situation. Of course, I may embellish the description or alter it ever so slightly to support the rightness of my position to my friend, who naturally agrees with me. At an organizational level, a sure sign of chronic chaos is when the rumor mill is the best source of accurate information. The gatherings around the proverbial water cooler used to be the Grand Central Station for gossip, but increasingly, the virtual water cooler on social media has supplemented the exchange and increased the potential for a rant to go viral.

When individuals are covert about their complaints or disagreements, a culture of pretense or pretending pervades. If I do not have the emotional courage to deal directly and openly with a person or group that is the source of my concern, I am left no other choice than to be two-faced and act as if everything is fine.

The primary bonding factor within these subgroups is an agreement with a given point of view or philosophy, at least on the surface. In organizations and groups, chaos takes many forms. Operating in a competitive society further reinforces the dynamics of chaos. A surefire way of recognizing that an organization is in chaos is the existence of cliques, camps, or subgroups. These cliques are formed based on sameness, agreement, and exclusion. People are either in or out. Cliques and camps reinforce "us and them" thinking, coupled with the other two tenets that construct divides: righteousness and the desire to conquer or overpower. Sometimes, it is as simple as the in-group and everyone else. Usually, it is more complex and parallels the structure of an organization and its various departments or divisions.

In recent years, there has been much discussion about the downside of silos and stovepipes within organizations, including the government. The working assumption, albeit unconscious, is that the interests of our group are primary. Somehow, the bigger picture gets lost in the process. The essential nature of cliques is tied to the act of exclusion. At the extreme end of the spectrum, cliques become cults. Cliques hurt people. One only needs to return to memories of the years in high school to recall the pain of being rejected by a clique or rejecting someone else who didn't belong.

Another telltale sign is a focus on others. Others may mean management, the other party, the president, the leader, another department, a parent, the government, or "those people." While the other may have a part to play in each circumstance, a focus on forces outside of oneself is a way of avoiding a look in the mirror. The focus on others can easily shift to blame. Someone or a subgroup is to blame for a mistake, a problem, a change, a bad decision. Blame goes beyond simply holding someone responsible for an action by adding the judgment that an individual or a group is bad, wrong, and morally irresponsible. The flip side of blaming is self-righteousness.

The focus on others also takes on a different form during a prolonged period of chaos. This form is so socially acceptable that very few question it, yet it often feels quite uncomfortable. On the surface, giving advice and helping others is usually well-meaning, but it's also usually misguided. It is one thing if I ask for advice and help. It is quite another if you presume that you know better and that I need to be fixed. Giving gratuitous advice and helping seem to be more benign than blaming and judging, but their effects can be equally troubling.

One of the neighborhood restaurants I frequent is a mom-and-pop sort of a place that struggles with getting all the parts of an operation to work together, sometimes at the expense of the customers. Regardless, my friends and I are regulars and usually are forgiving about the occasional slow service. A few months ago, the owner had opted to offer a Groupon, a coupon with a discount for the Friday dinner special. Our group happened to make a reservation on the last evening before the Groupon expired. Although we were seated on time, it took over an hour for our meals to arrive, and one of them was entirely wrong, so we all ate while one person drank wine, waiting for the delayed meal. Another person in our party became indignant and decided to take on the owner. The scene was rather uncomfortable. As the owner stood at our table and made an unconvincing attempt to apologize for the delay, she blamed the problem on Groupon. It had nothing to do with the kitchen or the wait staff or anything else. In that moment, in that circumstance, in that chaos, she truly did believe that it was Groupon's fault. (PS. It took us a few months to go back to the restaurant.)

When a group or relationship is experiencing chaos, those differences seem threatening. The reality of differences is part and parcel of life itself; without those differences, life on our planet would be boring.

Chaos in organizations is uncomfortable. Emotions erupt, but usually, they go underground. Chaos, although challenging, provides several self-protective features. Cliques or subgroups that form among trusted coworkers can be lifesaving in a toxic or dysfunctional workplace. I have been part of mergers and acquisitions, and felt the fallout from the clash of two corporate cultures. Ministers or executives are dismissed or pushed out, only to reveal that the group's problems ran deeper than the leader.

A group in chaos is difficult to lead because leadership is resisted, either overtly or covertly. In this stage, leaders can easily become scapegoated and blamed for the problems in a dysfunctional system. Other features of an organization in chaos include low morale and dissatisfaction of its members. People feel unappreciated and undervalued.

In a chaotic climate, meetings are unproductive, resulting in decisions that unravel as soon as everyone walks out the door. What is not said and withheld from the discussion can prove to be as unconstructive as expressed opinions that may offend or hurt people. If there is agreement about anything, it is that the situation is not working. Frustration runs high. Listening is particularly difficult because words must penetrate layers of judgments and distrust.

To address chaos in organizations, leaders most often attempt to organize out of chaos by restructuring, letting people go, or reorganizing to address the problems. Unfortunately, without addressing the underlying causes of the chaos, reorganization rarely is effective. People are fired or quit and seek greener pastures or pursue other opportunities. In organizations, intense chaos may surface occasionally, but in most situations, it is more like a low-grade fever that makes people feel lousy and gets in the way of getting things done.

There are few metrics for measuring the cost of chaos objectively, but few would disagree that the cost of low productivity, poor communications, stalled projects, replacing the casualties, and training new people is too high. Consider the following alarming statistics:

- A 2017 Gallup poll of millions of people from two hundred countries showed that "work is more often a source of frustration than fulfillment for nearly 90% of the world's workers."
- The same poll found that 70 percent of people in the United States are unhappy at their jobs.
- Overall, Gallup found that only 15 percent of workers feel engaged by their jobs. "Engaged" means they feel a sense of passion for and deep connection to their work, spending their days "driving innovation and moving their company forward."
- 62 percent of workers are described as "not engaged," meaning they are "unhappy but not drastically so." 23 percent are what Gallup calls "actively disengaged," meaning "they pretty much hate their jobs. They act out and undermine what their coworkers accomplish."
- In a 2017 Mind the Workplace survey, conducted by the nonprofit group Mental Health America and the Faas Foundation, 71 percent of seventeen thousand US workers in

nineteen industries said they were so unhappy with their jobs that they are looking to change employers.

- 63 percent of those surveyed in the Mind the Workplace study said that the stress of their job had "a significant impact on their mental and behavioral health." 66 percent of respondents said they "sometimes, rarely or never" feel like they can trust their colleagues to support them at the office.
- A *Harvard Business Review* survey reveals 58 percent of people say they trust strangers more than their own boss.

In chaos, the collective mindset has concluded that "this isn't it" or "this isn't working." Leadership is flawed. Decisions are poor or take too long or do not use an effective process. These work conditions have generated many cynical analogies: "We're like mushrooms. They keep us in the dark and feed us shit." Murphy's Law seems to prevail: "If something can go wrong, it will."

Chaos is also filled with polarities, each struggling to overcome its opposite. Invariably, within the nest of negativism, there will be a few optimists who try to convince their colleagues to look on the bright side or to see the glass as half-full, not half-empty. The Pollyannas in the group are, at best, brushed aside and, at worst, ridiculed.

About the time I first learned there was a term for the work I was doing—community building—I was a member of an executive management team in a newly formed large joint venture between two Fortune 500 companies. We were still in the early stages of the new company, and one of my areas of responsibility was strategic planning. At a management team meeting, I naively suggested that we should develop vision, mission, and values statements for the company. With a swift blow, the CEO quickly obliterated my recommendation and any credibility I had with his response: "Yes, Missy, we all know that you have two feet firmly planted in the clouds." Wow. So much for optimism. PS. The company, which was poised to go public in two years, failed and was sold to another company. Luckily, I bailed out in time.

A great deal of judgment and blame stems from these polarities. Accountability is an essential element of a mature (enlightened, self-actualized, high performing) individual or organization, but blame under the guise of accountability obscures the whole truth. If people who are part of a group engage in finger-pointing, it is a sure sign of chaos. Either literally or figuratively, finger-pointing is a gesture that suggests shooting.

Blaming others is always an incomplete truth because it oversimplifies complex circumstances and situations. Certainly, there are exceptions in which people are fully responsible and accountable for their actions.

Pointing out and naming an action is not blaming. What hurts and leads to deeper conflict and separation into sides is judgments. The acceptability of judgmental thinking is so pervasive in society that it's difficult to take issue with what seems such a natural characteristic of human beings. Throughout the years of community building work, I have come to realize that judgment and the blame and shame that accompany it are the beginning of violence against others.

Chaos in Society

Over the span of time, chaos at the societal level is likely more the norm than the exception. My first conscious awareness of societal chaos emerged when I immersed myself in learning about the French Revolution. I had learned about the Civil War, world wars, and other global conflicts in school, but when I dove into the Reign of Terror, the guillotine, heads paraded on pikes, and years of turmoil, I imagined what it must have been like as chaos erupted. Often, chaos in society remains in the background, pervasive but low key. Periodically, chaos is in the foreground and impossible to ignore.

We happen to be living through a period that provides an up-close-and-personal look at chaos at the societal level. Regardless of one's political persuasion, most would agree that acute chaos played out daily in both the domestic and global arenas in the aftermath of the 2016 US election and during the Trump presidency. Within a month of the inauguration, the threat of nuclear attacks moved to the front burner. I am reminded of Dr Peck's prophetic words at the beginning of *The Different Drum*: "I am scared for my own skin. I'm even more scared for the skin of my children. And I am scared for your skins." At the end of the four years, pure chaos reigned during the January 6th assault on the US Capitol.

The rise in mass shootings is pure chaos. Controversy about immigrants—and the desire to exclude people from other countries—is chaos. A revolving door of White House officials, with many being thrown to the curb, became normalized chaos.

Even the term "chaos" was a daily utterance by the media. Like all chaotic times, it was painful, tumultuous, and replete with feelings of frustration and despair. A therapist friend of mine recently mentioned that nearly all his clients bring their thoughts and anxieties about the Trump presidency into their therapy sessions on a routine basis. We witnessed classic chaos of a massive stale. Examples include Trump's insistence on "my way or the highway," demeaning name-calling (Little Marco, Lyin' Ted, Crooked Hillary, Little Rocket Man, Sleepy Joe, Mini-Mike), building walls to keep bad people out, constant blaming, shaming, firings, resignations, and finger-pointing.

The last time I worried about nuclear war was during my childhood in the 1950s, when all the neighbors were building bomb shelters. With the potential of nuclear war moving to the foreground, we are so far from a being a country, or world, that can transcend and learn from our differences. Dr. Peck's distress call is more relevant than ever. In these troubled times, chaos is fulfilling its function: to avoid the task of uniting the country and the responsibility of governing the nation.

The most basic and powerful force at work in chaos is the need and desire to control, which is tied to the exercise of authoritative power. It is next to impossible to get anything done when everyone wants to do things their own way. As in the community building circle, it is evident when a group is in chaos by the attention on how the other is to blame and the focus on attention. Chaos and narcissism go hand in hand, in that narcissists are largely incapable of stepping outside their own point of view and seeing from others' perspectives. So it is in chaos when tempers flare and conflicts simmer and boil.

Emptying in Relationships and Families

With the preponderance of chaos, people are so busy protecting themselves that personal emptying usually takes place as a personal process or in small pockets of trusted people who provide a safe environment for vulnerability, such as group therapy, support groups, 12-step meetings, bereavement groups, or cancer support groups. In relationships, the capacity to empty, to let go of hard feelings, and to reveal vulnerability is essential to develop a healthy relationship. Most people stumble into the process of emptying through trial and error. Some learn by working through a crisis in a marriage—an affair, an addiction, an incident of abuse. Ephesians 4:25–26 speaks of the importance of emptying: "Wherefore putting away lying, speak every man truth with his neighbor: for we are members one of another. Be ye angry, and sin not: let not the sun go down upon your wrath."

In retrospect, I would not have the experience of family I have today without learning about emptying through community building. I have been divorced twice. The first divorce, at age twenty-eight, was easy. We even used the same lawyer and continued our relationship for a year after the divorce. The second divorce, at age forty-two, after two children, was hard, especially during the times immediately after our separation and divorce. I felt so many unfamiliar emotions: anger, resentment, sorrow, grief. I alternated between blaming him and blaming myself. I buried all of it and moved on.

At a community building workshop some two years after the divorce, an innocent comment from another participant triggered a most unexpected and profound response in me. All the buried emotions I had been carrying erupted. Quite suddenly, I was moved to speak and shared my story. I do not remember exactly what I said, but the sorrow resurfaced in a way that seemed beyond my control. It simply had to come out. My sharing triggered a definite shift into a sense of community, as one person after another, touched by my story, shared their own regrets, losses, and grief. As we came to the close of the session, a young Methodist minister offered to hold a ritual at the lake at the conference center. I recall that the whole group joined in as he spoke gentle and healing words, and then, without any direction, the entire group waded into the lake. Our individual and collective sorrow was cleansed. In that moment, I realized I had been given the gift of forgiveness—for my ex-husband and for myself.

After that experience, my relationship with my ex-husband changed. We remained friends and celebrated holidays together. Now we both live alone, but close to my daughter's family and near our two amazing granddaughters. We travel together, share meals nearly every day, vacation as a family, and still love each other, despite our history.

Emptying in Groups and Organizations

Without realizing it at the time, I stumbled into the power of emptying in the workplace a few years before I experienced community building through FCE. When I first started consulting and facilitating in the late 1970s and early 1980s, I was introduced to and trained in Application Enabling, a process developed by IBM to develop computer systems rapidly. I facilitated dozens of group sessions, which typically took place over several days. One of the guidelines was for the group to identify all the issues they were facing in trying to address a business problem or need—billing, financial reporting, claims processing, inventory management. The key feature of the guideline was to simply identify the issue, without discussion and debate. Invariably, after the group caught on, hundreds of issues came spilling forth and were captured on large sheets of paper posted around the room. Sometimes, we ran out of wall space. Issues were identified until they stopped flowing, rather than having a set time allotment for the task. What one person said would prompt another thought, then another, and so forth. Then we turned to categorizing the issues, which required group consensus. In most cases, all the issues collapsed into between seven and ten categories. For each category, the group developed goals and tasks. Application Enabling used an emptying process for a very pragmatic purpose: developing specifications for complex computer software.

Each time I facilitated a session, the diverse group, which included the techies, analysts, business users, and executives, came together as an effective working group. In retrospect, they developed a sense of community through emptying issues affecting their work in an environment that was structured to foster listening.

When we train community building facilitators, in the middle of the five-day program, we watch *The Green Mile*, a 1999 film based on a Stephen King story. The film is a must-see for anyone interested in community building or facilitation.

The story centers on the prisoners and guards on Death Row, known as the Green Mile—the pathway to the electric chair. Tom Hanks plays the lead role of Paul Edgecomb, who oversees the execution unit and is forever changed by one of his charges, John Coffey. We use the film to illustrate how the principles of community building can be integrated into even the most unlikely settings. The film captures the struggle between good and evil, the impact of treating people with extraordinary respect, how to establish a safe environment in volatile and difficult circumstances, and being open to Spirit.

Paul Edgecomb empties himself of his preconceived notions of John Coffey, an enormous African American man who was convicted of murdering two young girls. As a series of events unfolds, Paul concludes that John is, in fact, innocent. "Why, I don't think he did it at all," he declares. Paul personally experiences John's healing powers, and he and his fellow guards witness John bringing Mr. Jingles, an inmate's adopted pet mouse, back to life. By letting go and recognizing John's gifts, Paul trusts his experience of John and takes a huge risk, resulting in a miraculous healing involving the warden's wife. The film illustrates so many other community building lessons, including creating a safe space, letting go of preconceived notions, working as an effective group, and the power of truth-telling and storytelling. And perhaps a sense of community is present because of the omnipresence of death on the Green Mile. Death somehow always brings a new appreciation for life.

Community in Daily Life

My experience working with families, groups, and organizations has shown that most people have felt a sense of community some time, somewhere. A sense of community tends to be fleeting, like an apparition that serves as a reminder of a force greater than we can understand. These experiences are few and far between, but when they occur, they are accompanied by a sense of gratitude and reverence. The best case scenario is to establish, then maintain a sense of community as the foundation for families, organizations and society.

Changing the Foundation

Ultimately, the audacious goal of *Building True Community* is for more people to experience a sense of community, more of the time. If people were able to learn and apply what it takes to build a sense of community and put that knowledge and skill in practice everywhere, I believe our world would be better. To accomplish such an ambitious goal, our systems and structures will require transformation.

In chapter 3, the stages of community building were portrayed with four symbols:

Stages of Community

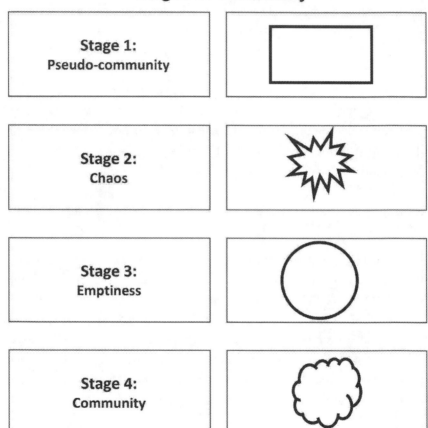

Stage 1: Pseudo-community	□
Stage 2: Chaos	✺
Stage 3: Emptiness	○
Stage 4: Community	☁

In most groups, pseudo-community is the default—the common denominator that operates as a foundation. Relating on the surface, playing it safe, and avoiding differences are the norm. Chaos is prevalent, either subtly or acutely, and is viewed as unavoidable and business as usual. Emptying and the resulting sense community may occur, but typically only with a few trusted people—certainly not in a group or team setting.

The diagram below summarizes such a group or organization:

Typical Organizations

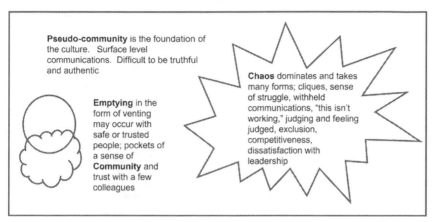

Pseudo-community is the foundation of the culture. Surface level communications. Difficult to be truthful and authentic

Emptying in the form of venting may occur with safe or trusted people; pockets of a sense of Community and trust with a few colleagues

Chaos dominates and takes many forms; cliques, sense of struggle, withheld communications, "this isn't working," judging and feeling judged, exclusion, competitiveness, dissatisfaction with leadership

An alternative is to do the difficult work of establishing a foundation of community. What that means is that a group has made a commitment to make changes in many of the fundamental ways people relate to each other. It means that a group has dedicated the time and energy to go through the community building process, either in an actual workshop experience or gradually over a period. In either case, the group has experienced a sense of community and learned the importance of dealing with differences and chaos through the discipline of emptying. Although difficult, people in the group have been able to reconcile conflicts successfully by practicing attentive listening, giving others the benefit of the doubt, being transparent about issues and perceptions, and demonstrating extraordinary respect. People have practiced these disciplines consistently with favorable results, so that people have learned to trust the process. When chaos does surface or erupt, individuals recognize that issues need to be aired and that restructuring or reorganizing alone will not provide resolution. Clearing the air is necessary.

Being in such a group is nurturing, stimulating, and safe, and it makes one feel radically alive and fully human. I believe that this should be our default, our norm. To change the foundation from pseudo-community and chaos to community, the principles and practices that govern community building are applied by the people involved, and new ways of being together are integrated.

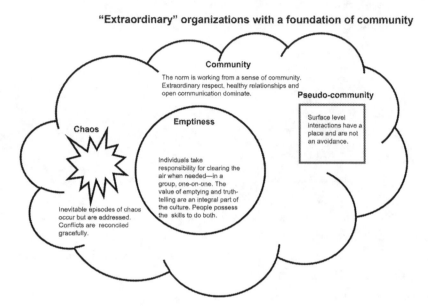

"Extraordinary" organizations with a foundation of community

Community
The norm is working from a sense of community. Extraordinary respect, healthy relationships and open communication dominate.

Pseudo-community
Surface level interactions have a place and are not an avoidance.

Chaos
Inevitable episodes of chaos occur but are addressed. Conflicts are reconciled gracefully.

Emptiness
Individuals take responsibility for clearing the air when needed—in a group, one-on-one. The value of emptying and truth-telling are an integral part of the culture. People possess the skills to do both.

Integration of Principles and Practices

FCE Mission

Not long after the Foundation for Community Encouragement was formed, I was asked to facilitate a planning session with the board of directors to develop a mission statement for the organization. I was new to the organization, having attended only a couple of workshops. I had met the chair of the board, Mary Ann Schmidt, at the first workshop I attended a few months previously, and she apparently saw that I might be helpful to the organization, given my years of experience with group facilitation.

We agreed that the entire group would need to reach consensus on the mission statement. To begin the process, I sent each individual out to be in solitude for a half an hour to create a personal mandala, using images of what the community building experience meant to them. When the group reconvened, everyone shared their images as I created a wall full of each word they spoke, recorded on Post-It notes, or as I refer to them, "yellow stickies." In a daylong conversation, the goal of consensus on the mission was achieved. Over the years, we have made some additions to the statement, as additional principles have been adopted as key to community building (the additions to the original statement are in bold):

> FCE encourages people, in a fragmented world, to discover new and better ways of being together. Living, learning, and teaching the principles of community, FCE serves as a catalyst for individuals, groups, and organizations to:
>
> - Communicate with authenticity
> - Relate with love and respect
> - Deal with difficult issues
> - Bridge differences with integrity
> - **Seek, honor and affirm diversity**
> - **Acknowledge our human frailties**
> - **Take responsibility for our actions and make amends where possible**
> - **Practice forgiveness for ourselves and others**
>
> FCE's approach encourages tolerance of ambiguity, the experience of discovery, and the tension between holding on and letting go. In our work to empower others, we remember our reliance upon a Spirit within and beyond ourselves.

The statement serves as a description of what happens over time to individuals, groups, and organizations that live and learn the principles of community. The mission statement describes how people might operate in a culture of community. In a community building workshop, through trial and error, participants learn how to create such a culture. Each guideline is rooted in a fundamental principle, or law, that establishes "ways of being together" that are nonviolent, mutually respectful, informed by reality, safe, and self-correcting. By applying the principles and practices of community building, it is possible for our families, groups, organizations, and institutions to become environments, or cultures, in which people experience acceptance, the freedom to be authentic, continuous learning, and an ability to reconcile conflicts without harm.

Community Building with Oneself

Community building with oneself is not as strange as it may sound. Many times, I have been conflicted about a decision, about a relationship, about an issue at work. Even sitting in a community building circle requires a degree of internal community building. Looking back, I have used journaling to get a clearer picture of my internal process. Another simple way is list-making by answering the question, "What do I need to let go of to achieve my goal or to resolve this issue?" Spiritual practices come in many forms and are ways of attaining a sense of peace and wholeness within. Meditation and other mindfulness techniques have been shown to contribute improved well-being and integration.

When I think about community building with oneself, I am reminded of the last monk in "The Rabbi's Gift" story. "'Of course, the rabbi didn't mean me. He couldn't possibly have meant me. I'm just an ordinary person. Yet supposing he did? Suppose I am the Messiah?' ... As they contemplated in this manner, the old monks began to treat each other with extraordinary respect on the off chance that one among them might be the Messiah. And on the off, off chance that each monk himself might be the Messiah, they began to treat themselves with extraordinary respect."

Community Building in Relationships and Families

On one occasion, I was recovering from surgery and was not able to purchase a card and gift for my father's birthday. So I wrote him a letter, telling him all the things I loved and appreciated about him. After the first paragraph, I instructed him to keep reading and just let it all in. After he read it, he called, and we both ended up sobbing on the phone. After he died fourteen years later, my sister and I were sorting through all the belonging in our family home. In the desk drawer next to his side of the bed, I found the folded letter, nearly falling apart from being opened and closed so many times. I am thankful for the surgery that facilitated an opportunity to connect so deeply with my dad.

In the early days of FCE, we would hold invitational workshops to introduce our organization to our circles of family, friends, and colleagues. I will never forget traveling by car from Cincinnati to Knoxville with my parents. The journey itself was an adventure as a result of driving through heavy fog for what seemed like hours. Finally, the sun burned off the mist as we approached Knoxville, and we spent three days together in the community building circle. We spent hours after each session talking about what we were experiencing, and in those days, we formed a friendship that transcended the parent-child relationship. After that, we were able to talk about anything and everything. To this day, I am grateful for the chance to be in the circle with my parents.

On several occasions, I have co-facilitated community building within families, including a family business. Admittedly, these sessions were among the most difficult but rewarding experiences. What emotional courage it took for members of a family to be together and surface old hurts, disappointments, and struggles. In the end, their bonds and love were strengthened, despite a history of challenging issues and interpersonal conflicts.

Although a community building experience is ideal, the purpose of this section is to point out ways that the principles and practices can be applied outside the circle. As a place to start, consider keeping a personal log of your close relationships with family and friends. What stage does each relationship operate in? What old judgments are you carrying? What communication have you been withholding? What would it take for the relationship to go deeper and be more authentic? Is it even worth it to risk emptying?

Another starting point is to pay attention to you statements and their effects. Then try implementing I messages. Set aside some time to have a heart-to-heart conversation with the individuals you would like to be more connected with.

If you are brave and adventurous, plan an event or expedition that takes you, along with close friends or family, beyond your comfort zone and invites the unknown.

Community Building in Ongoing Groups and Organizations

For most people, it is rather impractical to convince their family, organization, or country to sit in a circle and build community, as in the community building model. Over the years, in the work with community building in organizations through FCE as well as in my own consulting practice, we have sought to infuse community building principles and practices into the life of organizations. Inherently, when organizations describe the values they aspire to, the values are usually aligned with the values of community building. In most instances, despite the rhetoric espoused by an organization, it is very difficult to live the values on a day-to-day basis. Simply declaring the desire to be open and honest, have integrity, be committed to customer service, collaborate with partners, be committed to excellence and stewardship, or be committed to lifelong learning does not make it so.

In the work with community building in organizations, some groups participate in community building in a retreat setting. Community building workshops have taken place in a wide range of settings, including a manufacturing plant, a product distribution business, a large car dealership, a number of churches, the US military, an entertainment company, a software development company, dozens of nonprofit organizations, an international Christian organization, a family business, and a multisector environmental coalition. In such settings, a multistep process is needed. The first step is an assessment of readiness. The second step is a community building experience. We have found that the profound learning that results from community building requires reinforcement and follow-up activities to achieve systemic change. The principles, practices, and new behaviors must be integrated into the organizational culture to sustain the positive benefits of community building. Complex systems that permeate the organizational structure need focused attention to adjust to a new set of norms.

In retrospect, I wish FCE had developed the capacity to track the lasting impact of community building over time, but the organizational work was always secondary to the primary community building workshops. As I began working on *Building True Community*, I did reconnect with a few people who were still associated with the organizations that made significant investment in integrating community building practices into the culture.

One of the groups is Henry's Fork Watershed Council in Idaho. The Watershed Council began in 1993 as an initiative of the Henry's Fork Foundation to build trust and to find a way to collaborate, solve problems, and open lines of communications among the various stakeholders in the watershed. Jamie Laatsch, the foundation's communication director, said the foundation experienced a personality change in the early 1990s by shifting from an adversarial approach to a program-based collaborative approach. Today, the council describes itself as a "grassroots community forum that uses a nonadversarial, consensus-based approach to problem solving and conflict."

During the early days of its formation, the council membership participated in an FCE-facilitated community building workshop, which still has a lasting impact. Some twenty-seven years later, the council still begins its meetings with two minutes of silence and a community building circle, a tradition at every meeting since its inception. The council also uses co-facilitators.

In a 2019 article in the *Idaho Falls Post Register*, Mike Lawson, one of the founding members of the Henry's Fork Foundation and a general manager of Henry's Fork Anglers, a store and guide service in Island Park, stated that the Henry's Fork Watershed Council is one of the foundation's greatest accomplishments:

> *"This watershed council has been able to establish a situation where all the users groups and the management agencies were all able to sit in the same room and discuss all kinds of different levels of concern with regard to the river,"* Lawson said. *"To see the level of communication and trust that exists today compared to the old days is honestly just astounding."*

Another example of a company that chose to utilize community building in a business setting is Carlisle Motors, an automobile dealership in the Tampa-Clearwater area in west Florida. Scott Wilkerson, the former CEO, had attended a community building workshop and took a bold step in engaging the entire workforce of the multisite dealership in a series of workshops. To foster the application of the values and skills learned in the workshop, the company distributed "Principles of Community" that asks employees to "relate with love and respect" and to be "open to Spirit." Phil Mirvis, a management consultant and author who served on FCE's board, writes about the impact of community building in a chapter in *Leadership Perspectives*. In "Soul Work in Organizations," Mirvis recounts how "several community building workshops among staff are credited with 'breaking down the walls' between the sales force and back office and with humanizing working relationships throughout the auto dealership. Taking the principles to market, the dealership has adopted a 'fair and simple' approach to auto pricing, that eliminates 'haggling' and the disadvantages incurred therein by women and minorities in new and used car purchases … According to Scott Wilkerson, this is simply a matter of 'living the principles.'"

Adapting the Process for Organizational Settings

A systems development department in a large company is a most unlikely place to discover a sense of community. But some years back, before I knew of Scott Peck or FCE, I was fortunate to be involved in a project where we stumbled into sustained community. There were two computer system departments responsible for creating and maintaining a company's large mainframe systems for billing, reporting, client management, and other functions. One group, Advanced Technologies, had the responsibility of building state-of-the-art systems using the latest technologies. The second department, Systems Maintenance, was relegated to writing tedious code to maintain existing systems, including quick fixes to programs, developing add-on modules, and running many reports.

I was asked by the newly appointed department head of Systems Maintenance to help him address many issues in the group he had inherited. He had a sense that underlying concerns were affecting morale and performance. We launched the "People Issues Project" to engage everyone in the department to identify and dissolve these barriers. The project began with a series of facilitated retreat sessions that included a mixture of people at all levels in the department. Each session lasted two full days. At the beginning of each session, I introduced set of simple guidelines to encourage listening, candor, and interaction.

The first step in the process encouraged participants to put issues on the table. I defined issues as anything that was bothering anyone about the department and how things were working. The guideline for this part included an instruction that participants simply identify issues using a modified brainstorming approach—issues were not discussed or debated. As the facilitator, I captured each issue on large sheets of paper and posted them around the room.

The issues identification step took almost an entire day in each of the five groups we conducted. In each session, people began by speaking about issues in general. "There are communication breakdowns," or "We don't do a good enough job with planning for projects." However, as each group progressed, the issues became more specific, more personal, and more honest. Many participants admitted that they felt like second-class citizens because Advanced Technologies got all the good projects. As soon as one person spoke up, another would build on it and take the issue deeper. Individuals began speaking about their disappointments, difficulties working in their project teams, and the impact of changes in the company, which had just experienced its first downsizing after a long history of being a lifetime employer.

With so much focus on work tasks, people in the department had little time to discuss emerging conflicts or other communication challenges. The retreat sessions provided the group a chance to listen to each other, connect, and realize that they were not alone. As one person said, "I had no idea that other people felt the same way."

As individuals continued to share their hurts in the workplace, a sense of calm, tenderness, and mutual respect spread over the room—a real sense of community. As one person put it, "I just don't feel appreciated here at all." The sessions gave people a chance to connect to each other more deeply, share concerns, and shape the kind of organizational culture they wanted to have.

In the end, we had more than a thousand individual issues listed from each of the five sessions involving a hundred and fifty employees. When all was said and done, all the issues boiled down to a handful of topics: communication, teamwork, planning, morale, appreciation, professional development. To address the people issues, we formed a steering group and committees that tackled each of the issue areas to make improvements.

One of the committees, the Appreciation Committee, decided to hold a workshop open to all members of the department. Each person received a handwritten, personal invitation to attend—no memo, no generic announcement. I facilitated the workshops, which explored how appreciation is a lost art form, discussed barriers to giving and receiving appreciation, and identified guidelines for how to express appreciation. We discussed how individuals have a hard time accepting compliments because there is often a motive behind a compliment, so they are naturally resisted. Yet, so often, people feel unappreciated. I then went on to define how important it is for people to express genuine appreciation of others.

Next, we defined genuine appreciation: it is best done when it is specific, timely, descriptive, truthful, and without motive. Most of the people in the department had worked together for many years and had much history together. After learning about barriers and how-tos, in the last part of the workshop, people practiced providing and accepting statements of appreciation. The result was surprising and powerful. People's hearts opened, they felt valued, and each person's unique gifts were acknowledged. After the first workshop, we made sure we added tissues to the list of workshop supplies. People left on a real high—another taste of community.

The People Issues Project resulted in dramatic changes in the department by creating and sustaining a sense of community in the workplace. In the end, the department established a kinder, gentler, high-performing miniculture within a large corporation. Word of mouth spread, and the project was highlighted in a progressive journal covering workplace issues and innovations.

Values and Community

For some forty years, I have listened to people from all sorts of organizations, agencies, businesses, and companies express a longing for a workplace that walks its talk and practices the values it preaches. Yet people spend most of their waking hours over the course of a lifetime at work. It only makes sense that life would be better and healthier for everyone if workplaces experienced a sense of community. It is not surprising that many of the most common corporate values are similar to community building principles. Consider the following list of values that show up over and over across all sectors:

- authenticity
- honesty/truthfulness
- trust
- accountability
- attitude of service
- humility
- continuous learning
- constant improvement
- diversity
- quality
- teamwork
- collaboration
- team member growth and happiness
- caring about our communities

Research has demonstrated the link between core values and long-term sustainability of companies. In *Built to Last: Successful Habits of Visionary Companies,* Jim Collins and Jerry Porras discovered two common abilities among companies that endured for at least 125 years: preserving its core (values, purpose) and stimulating progress (innovation). Like habits, values are learned and practiced consistently.

Making values real rather than simply rhetoric is difficult and necessary work in an organization.

Using Modified Guidelines

Although there are exceptions, community building guidelines are perceived as too unstructured, process-focused, and, frankly, strange by organizational leaders and managers. Over time, I have developed a modified set of guidelines that introduce the principles and practices into a facilitated session. A practical way to integrate community building principles and practices into an organizational setting is to use these guidelines in shorter, multiple sessions over a period of time. The following is a list of guidelines I often use in meetings or group sessions that attend to both the process and the task to be accomplished:

- Be present.
- Listen attentively.
- Speak for yourself; use I statements.
- Monitor your own airtime.
- One at a time; let others finish.
- Tell the truth.
- Put issues and ideas on the table.
- "But" shuts down conversation; "and" opens it up.

Being present refers to physical and emotional presence, which serves to stress the importance of staying in the room as well as paying full attention. While describing the guideline "listen attentively," I show the group the Chinese character for this word, which includes the characters for "ear, "you, "eyes, "undivided attention," and "heart."

To Listen

Speaking only for yourself and letting others finish their statements creates a climate of mutual respect. The two guidelines that point to emptying (without introducing the term, per se) are "tell the truth" and "put issues and ideas on the table." Recently, two popular management books, *Radical Candor* and *Managerial Moment of Truth*, promoted the use of truth-telling as a tool for improving performance. To provide a pathway for moving through chaos, the "'but' and 'and'" guideline encourages acceptance of others' ideas and diffuses the notion of right and wrong.

People in the workplace who attend or sponsor team building and planning retreats for their organizations report dissatisfaction with the variety of icebreaker and other contrived activities that attempt to orchestrate the group to achieve its task. The most common feedback is that the activities are "hokey" and "simplistic." Consultants and facilitators typically design these icebreaker and small group activities, and groups put up with them, only because they are in pseudo-community. By using the modified community building guidelines, groups can move directly into emptying the issues facing the organization. Since the issues are less personal than those people bring to community building workshops, it is easier to put them on the table. Unlike the community building process, information is recorded on large sheets of paper as people are speaking so the group can discern the themes later in the process.

Introducing a Taste of Community

On occasion, I have been asked to discuss community building at conferences or as a first step in introducing the concept to an organization. In these sessions, my aim is to tap into individuals' experiences of both chaos and community. The group forms pairs, and I indicate that during the activity, each person will reflect on and share about several situations. I ask that when one member is speaking, that the other listen without comment or questions.

In the first scenario, I ask each person to recall a time or place when they were with a person or in a group and really did not feel heard, understood, accepted, or appreciated. After about three minutes, I instruct the pairs to switch roles so both get a chance to speak.

Next, I gather the group's attention and ask them to call out some key words that describe what those experiences were like. Using a blue marker, I write down the responses on a flip chart. We go back to the pairs for the second scenario: Recall a time or place when you were with a person or in a group and really did not hear, understand, accept, or appreciate someone else. Again, pairs share, and I record the key words and phrases.

Invariably, the key words for these first two scenarios are similar: judged, criticized, hurt, angry, frustrated, dismissed, invisible, upset, discarded, annoyed, righteous, guilty. You get the idea.

Then we proceed through the final two scenarios: A time when you really did feel heard, understood, accepted, or appreciated by a person or a group, followed by a time when you were with someone and really understood, accepted, or appreciated that person. For the second set of experiences, I use a green marker.

The green scenarios are also similar: accepted, loved, warmth, not judged, connected, joy, bliss, affirmed, heard, respected, comforted.

To wrap up the first part, I pose the rhetorical question, "Where would you rather live, in the blue or in the green?" I ask the group to give a ballpark estimate of the percentage of time they are in the blue versus the green. At this point, I introduce the idea of community building to shift from the blue to the green. I suggest that the process helps people understand and develop the skills to make the shift deliberately.

In some cases, I go on to do a brief walk-through of the stages and may discuss the phenomenon of community by crisis versus community by design and the human longing for community.

Whenever I guide a group through this activity, I can feel a sense of peace and tenderness in the room as the pairs remember the green moments of community. It is a shortcut that uses past experiences of chaos rather than chaos in the circle, but it is an effective taste of community at a starting point for building interest in participating in a full community building experience.

Community Competencies

At the beginning of this chapter, I recounted how the mission statement for the Foundation for Community Encouragement was developed. The guidelines for community building were reviewed, with the suggestion that they offer sound guidelines for living outside the community building circle. Over time, with practice, the elements included in the mission statement evolved into competencies for effectively managing, perhaps even mastering, many aspects of relationships and life in general. Community building makes self-actualization accessible to more than the 1 percent of the population. In the description below, wording from the mission statement is italicized in bold.

Few would disagree that we live in a ***fragmented world*** and that part of life is learning how to cope with countless challenges without becoming overwhelmed and discouraged. Over the last several years, the concept of resilience has gained much attention. Resilience is the process of adapting well in the face of adversity, trauma, tragedy, threats, or significant sources of stress. Resilience is that ineffable quality that allows some people to be knocked down and pick themselves up and keep going, even stronger.

Through the experience of community building, individuals *discover new and better ways of being together,* including their capacity for resilience. Experiential learning is active and involves individuals in discovering and trying new skills and behaviors, coupled with reflection. The facilitators do not show participants how to build community other than providing the guidelines, so individuals must figure out what works and what does not work through experimentation. By *living, learning, and teaching the principles of community*, those doing the work of community building develop a set of skills and competencies. Some skills may develop immediately; others emerge and strengthen over time. In educational terms, these skills are learning outcomes. Perhaps a more accurate sequence would be learning, teaching, and living the principles of community. The principles are amazingly congruent with the principles set forth by the world religions and offer guidelines for living.

The community building experience is a *catalyst*. In chemistry, a catalyst is a substance that enables a chemical reaction to proceed at a faster rate than usual or under different conditions (as at a lower temperature) than otherwise possible. Beyond the chemical world, a *catalyst* is an event or person causing a change. The noun "catalyst" is derived from the Greek word *katalvein*, meaning "to dissolve." As described previously, the facilitators do not lead the group into community, but gently encourage them to pay attention to barriers to communication to be emptied or, in other words, dissolved. The work of community building does speed up the ability of *individuals, groups, and organizations* to apply these newfound competencies to become more effective, balanced, connected, productive, and peaceful.

A common theme in many of the groups and organizations I have worked with is the desire to be real and authentic, yet individuals seem to have a hard time doing so. In recent years, psychologists have identified the desire to be authentic—to act in a way consistent with one's values and sense of self, despite external pressures—as a prerequisite for well-being. When we *communicate with authenticity*, we engage in deep honesty and open connection with others. To be authentic is to be comfortable with vulnerability. Of all the takeaways from community building, the paradox that our strength rests in our vulnerability is one of the most surprising and enduring lessons.

The ability to relate with **love and respect** can sound like an unreachable goal, but participants routinely report the experience of "falling in love" with a group and the people in it. The themes of extraordinary respect and the power of acceptance are introduced early in the process. Gradually, as the consequences of judgments, biases, preconceived notions, and words that cause offense are played out and as individuals let go of these common barriers, people begin to feel safe enough to express themselves when moved. I often feel as if each person is a magnificent tapestry, with images and colors and beauty that needs a chance to unfurl. As people speak their truth, I am so often in awe of the inherent wisdom resident in the circle.

At one point in FCE's history, a member of the staff changed the wording in the mission statement from "relate with love and respect" to "relate with compassion and respect." I suppose it was felt that the word "love" might seem too soft or ethereal. Awakening compassion and empathy do occur during the experience, but love is a more accurate description of what people feel as their hearts open and form powerful connections with others. (PS. We restored the original wording.)

Given most people's propensity to confront the hard challenges in life, it is quite helpful to be able to **deal with**, rather than avoid, **difficult issues**. Neuroscience and expanded understanding about the power of our brains to rewire destructive patterns and create new neural pathways (more on this in the last chapter) have shown that as individuals become more aware of themselves and others, they lean into difficult problem solving rather than avoid it. During a community building experience, each group encounters a unique set of difficult issues; in most instances, they are resolved satisfactorily and, at times, elegantly.

One of the most difficult issues we face every day is dealing with differences, which can easily lead to miscommunications, misunderstandings, and conflicts. Left unresolved, conflicts escalate and build on earlier misunderstandings. Conflicts may evolve into polarization, division, and ultimately some form of warfare. It is possible to **bridge differences with integrity**. To do so requires the willingness to listen to other points of view and understand the perceived realities of others involved in the situation. It requires an appreciation that situations in which differences collide have multiple causes. Above all, it requires patience and a tolerance for messiness and lots of grey areas. Few situations involving differences are clear-cut or black and white. The word *integrity* in this context means being whole, undivided, and complete, not moral principles.

Some of the most challenging aspects of bridging differences calls upon us to realize our biases and prejudices related to racism, sexism, ageism, homophobia, and other "isms." One of the criticisms of community building early on was that workshops mostly attracted white people, which is understandable, as those attending workshops primarily came from reading Dr. Peck's books or attending his lectures. As the organization developed over time, workshops became more diverse, and whole new levels of learning began. I remember distinctly attending an FCE event in the early 1990s where a wise, powerful, and passionate African American woman, Pat Callair, directly confronted the contradiction implicit in an organization encouraging inclusivity. Pat brings a long history as a social worker on death row in South Carolina; she organized with Dr. King and is an accomplished therapist, an advocate for social justice, and an FCE facilitator. I do not recall her exact words, but she courageously called for the lack of diversity to be directly examined. Leadership of the organization listened, looked in the mirror, took the issue seriously, and realized that inclusion was not embedded fully in either the organization or in the mission statement. At the next meeting of the board of directors following the awakening, we amended the mission to include **seek, honor, and affirm diversity**. Our ongoing work on this principle and practice continues to this day.

Although I was not involved in the efforts, FCE-facilitated community building workshops played a key role in the truth and reconciliation work in South Africa during the dismantling of Apartheid.

Through funding from the Lily Endowment, FCE also facilitated a series of community building workshops with Jewish, Christian, and Muslim faith leaders.

If you are interested in delving into a deeper understanding of your acceptance of diversity and unconscious biases, visit the Project Implicit websites (https://www.projectimplicit.net and https://implicit.harvard.edu/implicit/). Project Implicit is an international collaboration between researchers who are interested in thoughts and feelings outside of conscious awareness and control. In addition to consulting services, lectures, and workshops on implicit bias, diversity, and inclusion, the group has developed a series of Implicit Association Tests (IATs) that uncover the "hidden, or automatic stereotypes and prejudices that circumvent conscious control." The project offers dozens of topics—race and ethnicity, religion, ability, class, gender and sexual identity, and more. When differences are coupled with implicit biases, the going can get tough and generate particularly challenging forms of chaos. Uncovering and rewiring such biases begins with self-awareness. Community building in a diverse group can be particularly powerful in revealing and beginning the emptying process. Experts also recommend making a conscious effort to develop cross-group friendships.

In 2009, several additions to the mission statement were adopted by the board of directors, which we renamed the leadership council. After twenty years of community building practice, those of us who had continued the work felt it important to acknowledge other principles and practices intrinsic to community building. We realized that capacity to be vulnerable is a critical element of the process, especially when entering the stage of emptying. So we added *acknowledge our human frailties.*

When I first encountered community building and Dr. Peck's description of emptying in a lecture and later in reading *The Different Drum*, I was struck by the emphasis on brokenness and how the admission of human suffering is a key ingredient for building a sense of community. It ran so counter to our culture, which emphasizes strength, competence, and obscuring our weaknesses. In a recent interview with Stephen Colbert by CNN's Anderson Cooper, the conversation wandered into how both had experienced tragic losses. In 1974, when he was ten, Colbert lost his father and two brothers in an Eastern Airlines crash. Anderson Cooper's father died during open heart surgery when he was also ten, and ten years later, his only brother committed suicide by jumping from the terrace of his family's high-rise apartment in New York City. As I watched the interview, it was clear that they had stumbled into community building. Toward the end of a lively interview covering a full range of topics, the conversation turned to the subject of grief and loss, something they shared.

Colbert's words still resonate with me. Cooper commented on a statement Colbert had made during another interview.

> **Cooper:** You told an interviewer that you have learned to—in your words—"love the thing that I most wish had not happened." … You went on to say, "What punishments of God are not gifts?" Do you really believe that?

> **Colbert:** Yes. It's a gift to exist. And with existence comes suffering. There is no escaping that. I guess I'm either a Catholic or a Buddhist when I say those things. I've heard those from both traditions. But I did not learn it, that I was grateful for the thing I most wish hadn't happened. Is that I realized it. And it is an oddly guilty feeling.

> **Cooper:** It doesn't mean you're happy about it.

Colbert: I don't want it to have happened. I want it to not have happened. But if you are grateful for your life, which I think is a positive thing to do, not everybody is and I'm not always. But it is the most positive thing to do. Then you have to be grateful for all of it. You can't pick and choose what you're grateful for.

And then, so what do you get from loss? You get awareness of other people's loss, which allows to you connect with that other person, which allows you to love more deeply and to understand what it is like to be a human being, if it is true that all humans suffer.

And so at a young age, I suffered something, so that by the time I was in serious relationships in my life, with friends or with my wife or with my children, is that I understand that everybody is suffering. And however imperfectly, acknowledge their suffering and to connect with them and to love them in a deep way. That not only accepts that all of us suffer but also then makes you grateful for the fact that you have suffered so that you can know that about other people. And that's what I mean. It's about the fullness of your humanity. What's the point of being here and being human? If you can be the most human you can be, I'm not saying best because you're going to be a bad person and a most human. I want to be the most human I can be and that involves acknowledging and ultimately being grateful for the things that I wish didn't happen, because they gave me a gift.

There it was, right on CNN. A perfect example of the power of vulnerability, brokenness, and our human frailties and how they factor into our humanness and compassion for others.

The last two additions to the mission statement are linked to our frailties as well. Part of being vulnerable is to admit that we make mistakes. Alexander Pope, in *An Essay on Criticism*, said it well in 1711: "To err is human; to forgive, divine." I have learned to admit my mistakes, to do my best to take corrective action to rebuild trust, and to forgive myself. Like the other practices, it is not so easy **to take responsibility for our actions**, especially when others are hurt, and **make amends where possible.** I have learned to acknowledge my actions and learn from them, then not dwell on what happened. I cannot undo what was done, but I can admit what was done and its impact. I can change my behavior to ensure that I do not repeat the action. I can let go of the shame and embarrassment I feel. I can be patient when it takes time for trust in a relationship to be rebuilt. I can grieve, then move on if trust cannot be rebuilt and a relationship is lost.

The divine part is to forgive myself, or to forgive others when I am on the receiving end. In the end, the shame, anger, and resentment I carry only hurts myself. So we added **practice forgiveness for ourselves and others** to the mission statement.

 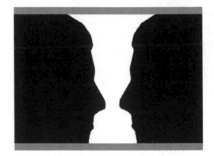

An old or young woman? Two faces or a lampstand? The images above are optical illusions. They invite a peek into the world of paradox.

The last section of the mission statement touches on some of the most unique abilities that stem from the work and how community building teaches how to appreciate paradoxes. The word comes from two Greek words, *para* and *dokein*, meaning "to seem contrary to."

Carl Jung stated that "paradox is one of our most valued spiritual possessions" and embodies "the conjunction of opposites." Life would be so much simpler and understandable if everything was clear-cut and made sense. So paradox can be hard to handle, as we try to wrap our brains around the tension of opposites. Paradox is everywhere. Despite scientific advances to gain greater understanding of the universe we inhabit, the totality is unknowable. We think of funny people, particularly social clowns and professional comedians, as being innately happy and good-humored. But often, the funniest people carry and repress deep sadness and use humor as a defense mechanism against darker emotions. Structure creates freedom. Oscar Wilde said he could resist anything but temptation.

The last part of the mission statement is my favorite. FCE *encourages the tolerance of ambiguity, the experience of discovery, and the tension between holding on and letting go.* It is unlikely that there is a college course out there or a how-to book on tolerance for ambiguity and balancing the tension between holding on and letting go, but I use both capabilities every day. Tolerance for ambiguity can be defined as the degree to which an individual is comfortable with uncertainty, unpredictability, conflicting directions, and multiple demands. Staying with the question can be invaluable and result in a better decision in the end. Recent research conducted at Brown University showed that individuals who are tolerant of ambiguity are more likely to cooperate with and trust other people.

The world is filled with far more ambiguity than certainty, yet little formal schooling focuses on how to accept, live with, and thrive from ambiguity. Acquisition of knowledge and expertise drives our educational systems and workplaces. For many, admitting "I don't know" is difficult, embarrassing, or even shameful. Decisions are rarely clear-cut. Making a good decision often requires the ability to be uncertain and not know what to do. Along the path to discovery, there are many an ambiguous or chaotic moment. I have no control whatsoever over ambiguity, over chaos, or over other people. It is better to able to tolerate ambiguity and be comfortable with not knowing. The willingness to not know opens the door to the experience of discovery.

Many years ago, I attended a two-weekend Est personal growth experience, popular at the time. I was in my early twenties and had just begun to dabble in my own spiritual journey, so the experience was eye-opening and transformative. At a point midway through the first weekend, I was reflecting on the source of my pervasive sense of guilt that seemed connected to everything but nothing specific. I had recalled a series of incidents, moving back in time to an earlier similar time, that I associated with this feeling of guilt. Suddenly, I was re-experiencing being a toddler, unable to speak. It was clear as day. I was watching my father sleep through the bars of my crib. I feel angry. I am very confused by this recollection.

In the workshop, I raise my hand to share this experience with the group. The trainer calls on me, and I begin to recount the story. About a minute into the story, I admit to my confusion that "I don't know what is happening."

The trainer interrupts me. "That's a change." It felt like a bolt of electricity running through my body. Here I was, standing up and sharing my story in front of a hundred people, and suddenly I feel totally exposed and vulnerable. He had seen right through me and my need to always "know what is happening."

There I was, on new ground, left with a feeling of being out of control, of not knowing, with the rug of certainty pulled out from underneath me. It was a life-changing moment.

I sat down, allowing the shock of the incident to subside. Then I discovered the incident that was the original source of my guilt. It was so simple but had such widespread effects.

My mother was working in a laboratory when I was a baby and toddler. My father was working on his doctoral dissertation and caring for me at home. Throughout my childhood, I had heard stories about "the accident" when I was about eighteen months old. I still have two scars on my inner thighs as evidence.

Back to the workshop. I am back in my crib, watching my dad sleep. I want him to wake up and play. I reach out through the bars and grab his matches from the table beside his chair. I had watched him strike them and make light. I wanted to show him how I could do it, too. In an instant, my gown is on fire, and I scream.

Indeed, he woke up. He lifted me, on fire, out of the crib and rolled me up in a small rug to put out the flames, then took me to the hospital.

What I realized as I re-experienced those moments was that I had lit the matches on purpose to get my father's attention. So all those times I heard about "the accident," something in me knew that was not true. It was no accident because I did it on purpose. Mind you, my eighteen-month-old brain had no way of knowing the consequences of playing with fire, but the net result was feeling guilty whenever I drew attention to myself. It was a major "ah-ha" moment.

The next day, I felt as though a ton of bricks had been lifted from my chest. Regardless of how it happened, I had my first conscious experience of emptying, of letting go. The guilt was gone.

Despite the importance of emptying and emptiness, neither word appears in the mission statement. I recall the significant debate about whether to include either word during the development of the statement more than thirty years ago. In the end, we chose to include the phrase "tension between holding on and letting go" instead. As described earlier, a critical requirement is for the facilitators to be empty and to let go of anything and everything that could be a barrier. As I have sought to integrate the principles and practices into my life, I deal with the tension between holding on and letting go daily. Over time, I find myself doing far more letting go than holding on, as I grapple with one of the central issues: the need to control.

Control is one of the most challenging for critical parts of the community building puzzle and the quest to live the principles. Control, on the surface, is usually viewed as a good thing. We work to have self-control and control of our lives to coexist in a civil society. In community building, the greatest source of conflict is the attempt to control others. I can influence or educate, perhaps. In the end, I am the only person I can control, and even that can be difficult, if I am being honest with myself. Admittedly, people possess varying degrees of self-control and discipline, but the number of people who have fulfilled all their New Year's resolutions is probably minuscule. I am like you and the rest of humanity in that I am an imperfect being, with my own set of frailties. In the spirit of tolerating ambiguity, I also have gifts and talents—some expressed, others dormant.

In a community building circle, the dominant feature of chaos is the repeated—and unsuccessful—attempts to fix, change, convince, or help others in the group. All these actions during chaos are forms of control. In chaos, most of the group's energy and attention is focused on what other people do (or don't do) or say (or don't say) and whether those words and actions are acceptable. Judgment of others prevails. Judgment, too, is a more subtle form of control. When people naturally withdraw and check out of the process (exclude themselves) rather than being emotionally present, it is a form of control. We can witness all the same patterns in life outside the circle.

As I have learned the power of letting go and letting be, I find myself with less and less need to control anything. I appreciate the AA Serenity Prayer, which speaks directly to the issue of control:

God grant me the serenity

To accept the things I cannot change;

Courage to change the things I can;

And wisdom to know the difference.

I would be remiss to imply that it is better to let go than to hold on. Recognizing that there is a tension between the two helps me keep my discernment muscles in shape. In the end, the things I value in my deepest self—the importance of family, being the best human being I can be, keeping an open heart and mind, fulfilling my purpose in life—are worth holding onto.

In writing this book, I have taken to heart the work of passing on valuable knowledge developed through the collective work of community building. For some thirty years, information about community building and facilitation has been transmitted orally at meetings, trainings, and community building workshops. Taking a stab at writing down the collective learning and wisdom from the work of FCE is a small step to **empower others**. Of all the guidelines, I believe the most powerful and mysterious one is to "speak when moved and do not speak when not moved." I have learned that one of the ways I know that I am moved is if a thought, story, remembrance, or emotion will simply not go away. Eventually, I recognize that I may be moved and proceed with what I have to say, even if I do not understand why I am sharing. Despite the stops and starts, the distractions and detours, I have known for a long time that I really do not have a choice about sharing what I have learned. I have also learned to trust the process and remember my **reliance on a Spirit within and beyond** myself. That same Spirit has just kept badgering me, relentlessly, until I stopped ignoring it and gave myself to the writing process.

Community Building as a Pathway to Transcendent Experience and Self-Actualization

I am not alone in affirming that living the principles makes life better on a practical level—less conflict, more authentic relationships, more peace of mind. But are there even additional longer term effects? Can community building as a practice lead to integration as a human being and development of group consciousness?

Throughout history, human beings have experienced an elusive phenomenon that crosses cultures and religions in which the individual perceives that human reality extends beyond the boundaries of day-to-day encounters. Regardless of the pathways to the extraordinary experience, the poets, mystics, philosophers, and ordinary people who have been fortunate enough to enter this extended reality characterize it in similar language: a sense of unity, joy, ecstasy, transcendence of space and time, illumination, awe, intense happiness, interconnectedness, harmony, well-being, affirmation of meaning and value of existence, uplifting, paradox, and transiency. These characteristics can all be used to describe a sense of community.

Abraham Maslow, the humanistic psychologist most famous for his hierarchy of needs and its end stage, self-actualization, named this phenomenon "peak experience" in his *Religious Aspects of Peak-Experiences* (1970), describing it as "feelings of limitless horizons opening up to the vision, the feeling of being simultaneously more powerful and also more helpless than one ever was before, the feeling of great ecstasy and wonder and awe, and the loss of placing in time and space." Maslow claimed that all individuals are capable of peak experiences. Virtually everyone, he suggested, has a few peak experiences in the course of their life, but such experiences often go unrecognized, are misunderstood, or are simply taken for granted.

Maslow argued that peak experiences should be studied and cultivated, so they can be introduced to those who have never had them or who resist them, providing them a route to achieve personal growth, integration, and fulfillment.

Since Dr. Peck introduced the concept of community building in the early 1980s, those who have experienced the process and the sense of community are hard-pressed to try to describe what happened to others. "Well, I guess you just had to be there," seems to be the way of acknowledging that it is nearly impossible to explain. Imagine trying to explain an orgasm to someone who has never experienced one. Dr. Peck discussed the close relationship between sexuality and spirituality in many of his writings and lectures. There also seems to be a parallel with how a group achieves a sense of community. The harder the group tries to achieve it, the more elusive it becomes. It is only after a sufficient period of friction and a willingness to let go that the transition period of emptiness makes way for the grace that accompanies community.

After nearly thirty years of empirical evidence from community building experiences all over the world, it is clear that the process is a relatively rapid pathway to the peak experience, or the transcendent experience, as it is called elsewhere. A principal characteristic of this experience involves transcendence of the differences that divide people and the dissolution of a primary conscious focus on or grounding in one's individual ego.

Others have also sought to describe what Maslow named peak experiences. Throughout the literature, there are two common themes that emerge. The first is that these experiences are brief and transitory. Maslow called them "transient moments of self-actualization." The second theme is the shift that occurs over time to what Maslow calls "plateau experiences," which is a characteristic of the self-actualized. He described it as a state of witnessing or cognitive blissfulness, the achievement of which requires a lifetime of long, hard effort and self-actualization.

In reading descriptions and research reports of transcendent experiences, there are parallels with Maslow's peak and plateau descriptions. Jeff Levin and Lea Steele describe the two types as "green" and "mature," and suggest there is a developmental continuum between the two.

The green type of transcendent experience is typically characterized as transitory and involving a profound experience of pleasure, oftentimes described as ecstatic. This may occur abruptly, in response to an event or specific physical or spiritual practice. It may be experienced in varying degrees of intensity. In some instances, it may be accompanied by unusual affective or perceptual phenomena. This type of experience may also occur repeatedly throughout one's life, depending on circumstances.

The mature type of transcendent experience, by contrast, is usually characterized as long-lasting. The feeling associated with the mature transpersonal experience is a more enduring serenity and equanimity. It is not so much about transient mystical feelings or phenomena as about entering a new state of awareness. It is more likely to be experienced as a self-transformational shift in one's consciousness or spiritual perception. This state of awareness parallels what Dr. Peck describes in *The Different Drum* as the last stage of spiritual development: "mystical, communal."

In addition to being a pathway to peak experience, people who are exposed to community building principles and practices over time may become self-actualized. The term became most prominent through Maslow's study of people who had the desire for self-fulfillment and realizing their full capabilities and potential. Maslow observed that "self-actualization ... rarely happens ... certainly in less than 1% of the adult population" (*Towards a Psychology of Being*, 1968). The fact that "most of us function most of the time on a level lower than that of self-actualization" he called "the psychopathology of normality." Maslow studied a host of individuals who seemed to be different, special, and extraordinarily human. In his studies, Maslow found that self-actualizers share similarities. Whether famous or unknown, educated or not, rich or poor, self-actualizers tend to fit the following profile:

- *Efficient perceptions of reality.* Self-actualizers can judge situations correctly and honestly. They are very sensitive to the fake and dishonest.
- *Comfortable acceptance of self, others, nature.* Self-actualizers accept their own human nature with all its flaws. The shortcomings of others and the contradictions of the human condition are accepted with humor and tolerance.
- *Spontaneity.* Maslow's subjects extended their creativity into everyday activities. Actualizers tend to be unusually alive, engaged, and spontaneous.
- *Task centering.* Most of Maslow's subjects had a mission to fulfill in life or some task or problem outside themselves to pursue. Humanitarians such as Albert Schweitzer and Mother Teresa are considered to have possessed this quality.
- *Autonomy.* Self-actualizers do not rely on external authorities or other people. They tend to be resourceful and independent.
- *Continued freshness of appreciation.* Self-actualizers seem to constantly renew their appreciation of life's basic goods. Time after time, a sunset or a flower will be experienced as intensely as it was at first. There is an innocence of vision, like that of an artist or child.
- *Fellowship with humanity.* Maslow's subjects felt a deep identification with others and the human situation in general.
- *Profound interpersonal relationships.* The interpersonal relationships of self-actualizers are marked by deep loving bonds.
- *Comfort with solitude.* Despite their satisfying relationships with others, self-actualizing persons value solitude and are comfortable being alone.
- *Nonhostile sense of humor.* This refers to the wonderful capacity to laugh at oneself. It also describes the kind of humor a man like Abraham Lincoln had. Lincoln probably

never made a joke that hurt anybody. His wry comments were gentle reminders of human shortcomings.

- *Peak experiences.* All of Maslow's subjects reported the frequent occurrence of peak experiences (temporary moments of self-actualization). These occasions were marked by feelings of ecstasy, harmony, and deep meaning. Self-actualizers reported feeling at one with the universe, stronger and calmer than ever before, filled with light, beautiful and good, and so forth.

In summary, self-actualizers feel safe, not anxious, accepted, loved, loving, and alive.

In Dr. Peck's *In Search of Stones*, he made the point that everything is "overdetermined." Rarely in his writings was he so vehement:

> *It is a great principle in psychiatry that all symptoms are overdetermined. This means that they have more than one cause. I want to scream this from the rooftops. "All symptoms are overdetermined." Except that I want to expand it way beyond psychiatry. I want to expand it to almost everything. I want to translate it, "Anything of significance is overdetermined. Everything worth thinking about has more than one cause." Repeat after me: "For any single thing of importance, there are multiple reasons." Again, for any single thing of importance, there are multiple reasons.*

Community, too, is overdetermined. Despite the attempt to provide as much information as possible about the process, the model, why it seems to occur, what to do to facilitate community, and everything else described in this book, in the end, no amount of words can truly replicate the unique splendor of community building. Even though some hundreds of thousands of people have participated in thousands of workshops, each one was unique and was overdetermined.

The most frequent way that community building is described uses an underlying developmental model. We describe the progression of the stages as a sort of life cycle that is quasi-linear, with the caveat that a given group will vacillate in and out of the stages. Another way community is described uses the metaphor of a physical journey. Groups speak about "reaching" community, as if there is a road to a destination. Both approaches acknowledge the requirement of time. I have heard all kinds of other metaphors over the years as people try to put the ineffable into words: Community as a spiritual discipline. Community as fruit salad. Community as cooking. Community as a birth process. All have a degree of truth but are incomplete. In one of my favorite books of all time, Donald Nicholl's *Holiness*, the author begins by acknowledging the absurdity of writing a book on holiness and then, in turn, expecting other people to read it after it has been written. He goes on to say that "this is meant to be a really simple, practical book in the quite straightforward sense that as a result of it ... a number of people will grow in holiness. ... One truly holy person is worth more than any number of books about holiness."

So when a group of people engages in the act of community building and their hearts and minds are etched forever by the gift of true community, it is worth more than any number of books on community.

When a group is in community, like other peak experiences, perception of time alters. There is a sense of the eternal present in the room. As my own understanding of community building has grown over the years, its eternal quality has become more prominent in my exploration of the mystery of community. From the perspective of being in community, the concept of a journey no longer seems adequate. Did the group really reach community, or was it present all along, but we could not see it? On a spring morning at sunrise, morning mist may obscure the landscape. Because I cannot see through the fog doesn't mean that the plants, trees, insects, and animals aren't there. As the sun's warmth burns away the fog, I begin to see all that was present all along. Perhaps community is a state of consciousness that is omnipresent, that is revealed to each of us as we burn away the layers of emotional, psychological, cultural, and ideological fog that block clarity and prevent connections. The next and final chapter, entitled "Beyond the Mystery," explores these questions in more detail.

A Group Self-Actualized

If individuals are capable of self-actualization, is it also possible that a group can do the same? One of the most remarkable features of a group in community is its ability to adapt effortlessly as its members interact and express themselves. Without instruction, without structure, people can tap into an innate sense of knowing what to do, how to respond, how to treat each other. This stage, which seems more like a state of group consciousness than a stage, is in sharp contrast to the awkwardness of pseudo-community and the distress of chaos. It seems hard to believe that it is the same group of people. Groups in community demonstrate many of the same characteristics of self-actualized individuals: a natural spontaneity, deep appreciation of others, a playful sense of humor, acute sense of connection and love, and comfortable acceptance of all members.

PART 4
CONNECTIONS

Genealogy of Community

My dad was insatiably curious, a useful characteristic for a scientist. After completing his doctorate in chemistry, he was recruited by Procter & Gamble and spent his entire career working for one company, a phenomenon almost unheard of today. But even the laboratory was insufficient material for his inquisitive nature. So he took up hobbies. Lots of hobbies. Building a pipe organ. The history of the English monarchy. Making furniture. Designing and building a doll mansion, with miniature bricks and furniture. Gourmet cooking. And genealogy.

We grew up hearing about the weekly discoveries from his ritual expeditions to the Cincinnati Public Library. Each week, he returned with new revelations, including names and histories of relatives like Patience Greenway and our favorite, Praise God Barebone. Long before computers and Ancestry.com, he traced our family back to the first European settlers who arrived on the *Mayflower*. He was the sole male among the bevy of elderly matrons that was the Cincinnati Chapter of the Society of Mayflower Descendants. On our road trips to visit the grandparents in Texas, we stopped at countless county courthouses so he could do more research, then made detours to crumbling cemeteries to make grave rubbings.

I, too, became infected with the need to know about the ancestry of all kinds—families, cultures, languages, and ideas. As my father's daughter, I would be remiss if I failed to devote attention to tracing the roots of community and the forces and people who influenced the community building model and its formation. Along the way, I have stumbled into many cousins of community that may or may not have had an impact on the FCE model. Together, these lineages reflect differences and commonalities associated with the phenomenon of community.

Like my father's genealogical discoveries, the overview of the roots of community explores places, times, and people who sought to pursue and describe community and its many meanings. It is a patchwork quilt of ideas rather than a linear progression.

One of the challenges of communicating about community is language. We use the word *community* to convey different types of community. I wish we had the benefit of many words for the various types of community like the Eskimos with at least fifty words to describe different kinds of snow. Perhaps if community becomes a more common experience, our language will evolve, and new words will evolve to describe everyday experiences. Oxford English Dictionary made *google* a valid transitive verb in 2006. In the meantime, we will have to settle for adjectives and phrases to differentiate types of community.

Physical Community

For most, community means a physical place—a neighborhood, town, or city. "My community" typically refers to where I live and does not include the notion of how connected I feel in that physical location. Community development is a broad term applied to the practices and academic disciplines of civic leaders, activists, involved citizens, and professionals to improve various aspects of local communities. It typically means revitalizing neglected and impoverished neighborhoods, homes, and businesses to improve the physical and economic well-being of a geographic area. People are mobilized through community organizing to act for needed change, which knits folks together for a common cause and introduces the notion of uniting for a common purpose.

Intentional Communities

Intentional communities are an extension of physical communities. Throughout history, there are many examples of intentional communities that formed as an alternative to societal structures. Intentional communities are groups of people who elect to live together in community, in a shared space, and conform to a set of idealistic shared beliefs and norms. Although the beliefs vary, what all intentional communities share is their separation from society.

Communal living in ashrams practicing Buddhist principles represents the most long-standing form of intentional community on record. In the fifth century BC, Gautama Buddha identified community, or *sangha*, as the third of the Three Jewels of Buddhism. Many intentional communities are centered around a spiritual practice or religious faith.

Examples include the Essenes (second century BC), early Christians (first century AD), Christian monasteries (AD 340), Anabaptists/ Hutterites/Mennonites/Amish (1525), Puritan colonies (1620), and the Shakers (1774). Although some no longer exist, most of these groups have changed over the years but continue today in some form.

Beginning in the nineteenth century a series of social experiments resulted in Robert Owen's New Harmony; Frances Wright's Nashoba; Brook Farm; Fairhope, Alabama; Degania Kibbutz; and Gould Farm. Findhorn Foundation and the communes of the 1960s and 1970s also explored communal living.

In the 1960s in Denmark, the cohousing movement was inspired by a newspaper article written by Bodil Graae titled "Children Should Have One Hundred Parents." As a result, in 1967, a group of fifty families organized a community project with a combination of individual housing and shared spaces; named Sattedammen, the oldest known cohousing community. A second organizer, Jan Gudmand Høyer, expanded the movement, drawing on his architectural studies at Harvard and interaction with experimental US communities. In 1968, he wrote the article "The Missing Link between Utopia and the Dated Single-Family House," which sparked the development of a second group. Cohousing has spread to the United Kingdom and the United States as well. In the 1990s, American architects Kathryn McCamant and Charles Durrett visited several cohousing communities in Europe, published *Cohousing: A Contemporary Approach to Housing Ourselves*, then went on to design American cohousing projects. The movement continues to grow slowly and is being seen in some circles as an antidote to loneliness. Vivek Murthy, the former US surgeon general, has called isolation the most common health issue in the country.

Social Community

Social scientists have debated how to define community since the beginning of the twentieth century. Community as a social phenomenon is relational and based on commonalities such as interests, skills, professions, artists, church, hobby, or politics. Robert Putnam, author of *Bowling Alone: On the Collapse and Revival of American Community*, focuses on the decline of "social capital." Putnam elaborates on the erosion of social interaction, particularly regarding participation in civic organizations, social clubs, and athletic associations such as bowling leagues. He claims the cause of this erosion is the rise of technology and its role in "individualizing" leisure time. In his second book, *Better Together: Restoring the American Community*, a follow-up to *Bowling Alone*, Putnam offers insight into the skills that build "belonging" and "identity." The skills—build safety, share vulnerability, and establish purpose—share much with the community building model. He makes it clear that it's far easier to build a community around "bonding" (commonality) than "bridging" (diversity).

> The problem is that bridge social capital is harder to create than bonding social capital—after all, birds of a feather flock together. So the kind of social capital that is most essential for healthy public life in an increasingly diverse society like ours is precisely the kind that is hardest to build.

Community Psychology

The field of psychology first introduced the term "sense of community." Seymour Sarason, who founded the Yale Psycho-Educational Clinic in 1961 and was one of the principal leaders in the community psychology movement, first presented the idea for academic study in 1974. Sarason discussed the phenomenon of the experience of community rather than its structure, formation, setting, or other features. Rather than describing a group of people living together according to shared principles, the psychological sense of community is "the perception of similarity to others, an acknowledged interdependence with others, a willingness to maintain this interdependence by giving to or doing for others what one expects from them, and the feeling that one is part of a larger dependable and stable structure" He defined sense of community as the feeling that one was part of a readily available, mutually supportive network of relationships upon which one could depend and as a result of which one did not experience sustained feelings of loneliness. Sarason believed that community was not a place but was everywhere. He maintained that the absence of community contributes to human misery and suffering.

Building on the work of Sarason, theoretician David McMillan and community psychologist David Chavis further advanced the theory of sense of community by describing four factors that work together to create that sense in their 1986 article, "Sense of Community: A Definition and Theory." McMillan and Chavis defined sense of community as "a feeling that members have of belonging, a feeling that members matter to one another and to the group, and a shared faith that members' needs will be met through their commitment to be together." The four factors that define sense of community— membership, influence, integration, and fulfillment of needs and shared emotional connection—have been the subject of extensive qualitative and quantitative research since the mid-1980s. Fellow community psychologists Branda Nowell and Neil Boyd added to the academic discussion by asserting that a sense of responsibility to one's community is an important aspect of the psychological sense of community theory and that there may be an indirect relationship between personal responsibility and well-being. The questions they raise are essential to completely understand community building: Is it enough simply to experience a sense of community as part of fulfilling human needs? Does needs satisfaction include a responsibility to others? Is community participation and engagement a choice or a human need?

Stages of Group Development

One of the most influential works on group development came from Bruce Tuckman, a well-respected educational psychologist. His classic 1965 article, "Developmental Sequence in Small Groups," defined the progression of groups through four stages: forming, storming, norming, and performing. In 1977, he added a fifth stage, mourning/ adjourning. Dr. Peck's discussion of stages parallels Tuckman's stages in many ways, with some fundamental differences. Most notably, Tuckman's third stage, norming, is described as the stage where the group is developing skills and agreeing on procedures for doing the work. Dr. Peck's third stage, "emptiness," represents a radical difference between the two models of group development. Tuckman's description seems to assume that the group somehow organizes itself and begins to build trust. In contrast, Dr. Peck insists that attempts to organize the group out of the second stage ("storming" or "chaos") only result in issues being temporarily suppressed or buried. For Dr. Peck, the only way out of a group's conflicts and dysfunction are "into and through emptiness." As a professional who has spent more than thirty years facilitating all sorts and sizes of groups in varied settings, Dr. Peck's pointing to the importance of self-reflection, taking personal responsibility, and "letting go of barriers to communication" is a major contribution to group theory.

In my own experience, no amount of norming helps a group transform itself into a high-functioning group or conscious, compassionate community. Most literature about stages of groups falls into one of two categories: social-relationship-oriented groups and task-oriented groups. The community building model bridges both.

Sense of Community

Of all the words associated with community, the term "sense of community" seems to convey the experience of community building best. September 11, 2001, when hijacked airplanes flew into the World Trade Center towers, the Pentagon, and a field in Pennsylvania, was a watershed event in countless ways. Before the gigantic wake-up call that changed life in the United States and beyond forever, the term *community* was almost universally interpreted in the geographic or territorial sense. Those of us who attempted to explain what happens in community building circles were met with puzzled looks and raised eyebrows. Post-9/11, it almost immediately became easier, perhaps because the entire country had just experienced "community by crisis," during which people spontaneously drop their suspiciousness of fellow humans; extend themselves to others; expose their vulnerability, fragility, and troubles; and feel connected. I recall standing in a line at Dunkin' Donuts when the first of the Twin Towers was hit, and the man in front of me, a stranger, turned to me and we hugged each other in an attempt to provide some modicum of comfort in the face of such unspeakable shock and fear. For some period, the ordinary rules of relating to others changed until people settled back into their isolation.

After 9/11, the term sense of community became widely understood and used. This remarkable shift was a tipping point that made it much easier to explain community building to others. In 2012, a Google search of the term "sense of community" yielded 77,900,000 references. In early 2017, it returned 312,000,000 results. In mid-2020, there were 1,330,000,000. At the time of this writing in mid-2022, there were 4,430,000,000 listings.

Scott Peck's Community Building Journey

As a psychiatrist, it is likely that Dr. Peck was exposed to the academic studies related to community as described above, but I have not been able to connect these branches to the Scott Peck "community family tree." In *The Different Drum*, he examined experiences that made up his "stumbling" into community, which I summarize here to add to the genealogy. Still, I suspect there must have been more influences than those he included in the book. I begin with describing known and documented influences, then turn to a description of other community connections.

Without publication of *The Road Less Traveled*, Scott Peck's first and most famous book, there would be no community building model or Foundation for Community Encouragement. In the late 1980s and mid-1990s, I spent much time at his home with him and his wife, Lily Peck, through my work with the foundation. I was living in Connecticut at the time, about an hour from their home on Bliss

Road overlooking Lake Warmamug, in northeastern Connecticut. The house was a sprawling farmhouse that stretched across their wooded property, with many cozy rooms well-suited for conversation, contemplation, and writing. He had written the book by hand on yellow legal paper in his study just off the kitchen, a practice he continued with all his writing. He completed the manuscript for *Psychology and Spiritual Growth* in the mid-1970s and received multiple rejections from several publishers, then Jonathan Dolger, an editor at Simon & Schuster, acquired the book in 1976 for $7,500 and renamed it *The Road Less Traveled: A New Psychology of Love, Traditional Values and Spiritual Growth*. After an initial printing of five thousand hardcover copies in 1978, with minimal promotion from Simon & Schuster, book sales grew steadily—mostly by word of mouth. After a helpful review from Phyllis Theroux in the *Washington Post*, *The Road Less Traveled* made the newspaper's best-sellers list and later the nationwide US best-sellers list for 598 consecutive weeks. Sales of the 1980 paperback edition began to double each year. By 1983, *The Road Less Traveled* showed up on the *New York Times* best-seller list and stayed there for a record-breaking 694 weeks—just over thirteen years—with more than ten million copies sold and translated into twenty-three languages. The *Guinness Book of World Records* lists it as the title with the longest life on the paperback best-seller list.

The runaway success of *The Road Less Traveled* changed life forever for Scotty and Lily. He hit the lecture circuit and spent months on the road, sometimes giving more than six lectures a week. After leaving his psychiatric practice to continue writing and lecturing, his active work on community building began. In *The Different Drum*, Dr. Peck wrote of the "longing" for community:

> On my lecture tours across the country the one constant
> I have found wherever I go—the Northeast, Southeast,
> Midwest, Southwest or West Coast—is the lack of—
> and the thirst for—community. This lack and thirst is
> particularly heartbreaking in those places where one

> might expect to find real community: in churches. …
> Yes, I am lonely … but I am infinitely less lonely than
> I used to be before I learned that is was human to have
> feelings of anxiety and depression and helplessness,
> before I learned that there were places where I could
> share such feelings without guilt or fear and people
> would love me all the more for it, before I knew I could
> be weak in my strength and strong in my weakness,
> before I had experienced real community and learned
> how to find it or create it again.

After significant research and experimentation, Dr. Peck arrived at a simple, but powerful approach for establishing a sense of community among a group of people by design rather than by crisis or disaster. *The Different Drum*, published in 1987 in the early days of his community building efforts, told the story of his encounters with the experience of community over twenty years, a description of the stages a group experiences, characteristics of true community, stages of spiritual growth, and potential applications of community principles. In the postscript of the book, Dr. Peck mentions the formation of the Foundation for Community Encouragement (FCE) with eleven other colleagues. As a tax-exempt public foundation, FCE was created to "encourage the development of community wherever it does not exist." In 1993, in a sequel of sorts, Dr. Peck followed with *A World Waiting to Be Born: Civility Rediscovered*. More philosophical, global, and Christian than *The Different Drum*, the second work on community building was less widely read and, in many ways, less accessible for those eager to learn the "how tos" of community building.

Fellowship of Alcoholics Anonymous (AA)

Dr. Peck acknowledged several primary influences on his development of the community building model: The Alcoholics Anonymous/12-step recovery movement, which he calls "the most successful community in this nation—probably in the whole world." Like community building, AA has its own ancestry. In the early 1930s, the cofounder of AA, Bill Wilson, was inspired by Edwin "Ebby" Thatcher, an old school friend and fellow alcoholic who became sober through his association with the Oxford Group. Frank Buchman, founder of the Oxford Group, a Christian organization, said, "The root of all problems were the personal problems of fear and selfishness ... [and] that the solution to living with fear and selfishness was to surrender one's life over to God's plan."

In the *Big Book of AA,* Bill W. recounts the story of rejecting his friend's offer to join the group to address Bill's alcoholism. Although Bill W. recognized Ebby's transformation, he held contempt for religion. Ebby's words planted the seed that would lead to AA: "Why don't you choose your own conception of God?"

"That statement hit me hard," Wilson wrote. "It melted the icy intellectual mountain in whose shadow I had lived and shivered many years. I stood in the sunlight at last. ... It was only a matter of being willing to believe in a Power greater than myself. Nothing more was required of me to make my beginning."

Ultimately, Bill W. did join the Oxford Group and stayed for several years before breaking away to form AA and write the first edition of the *Big Book* in 1939. In crafting the 12 steps, he began with the six tenets of the Oxford Group as raw material and then wrote out the first version of the 12 steps. Since its founding, dozens of other 12-step recovery programs, such as Narcotics Anonymous and Gamblers Anonymous, have spread throughout the world. An estimated 2 million AA members participate in more than 120,000 groups around the world.

Those seeking out AA are people in crisis, at a breaking point, who admit they are in need and can no longer go it alone. AA offers a safe place in which individuals can confess—and heal from—the reality of brokenness.

Aspects of the 12-step movement that were infused into the community building model include the use of names before speaking, reliance on a Spirit, the nonhierarchical structure (community is a group of all leaders), and respectful listening to individual stories.

Society of Friends

For anyone familiar with Quaker meetings, the community building circle will seem similar, at least at various points during the process. Of the many roots of the community building model, two core practices are clearly borrowed from the Quakers: the use of silence and the guideline "speak when you are moved to speak; do not speak if you are not moved to speak." Both seem odd and somewhat awkward at first during community building, but both are crucial for awakening self-awareness, stimulating authentic communication, building tolerance of ambiguity, and inviting spirit into the process.

Dr. Peck experienced Quaker meetings during his high school years. Much to his parents' dismay, at age fifteen, Scotty refused to return to his prestigious boarding school, Phillips Exeter Academy. He repeated his junior year at Friends Seminary in New York City's Greenwich Village, where he flourished both academically and socially. Despite individual differences and a wide range of different religious persuasions, he and his fellow students were "in truth, all 'Friends.'" The Quaker influence was pervasive, but not prescriptive in any way. During his two years there, he experienced his "first taste of community."

Wilfred Bion and the Tavistock Method

A third influence embedded in the community building model is the work of Wilfred Bion of the Tavistock Institute in Britain. As a psychoanalyst, Bion's most significant contribution concerned the understanding of group dynamics and viewing the group as an actual entity. Some dozen years after Dr. Peck experienced community at Friends Seminary, he attended a weekend group marathon with eleven other young psychiatrists, psychologists, and social workers in training at the army's Letterman General Hospital. Feeling that his experience with groups was lacking, he volunteered to participate in the first session facilitated by a senior army career psychiatrist, who had trained at the Tavistock Institute for Human Relations. The weekend session, which proved to be Dr. Peck's most intensive experience of what he later called "community," utilized the Tavistock Method.

During the course of a session, usually called a group relations conference, the group learns experientially that the group's agreed-upon task is accompanied by hidden dimensions, or "assumptions," that actually prevent the group from achieving the task. These hidden assumptions are dependency on a leader, flight/flight behaviors, and pairing (subgroups). Although the Tavistock Method is a powerful experiential tool through which group phenomena that are usually invisible become observable, it is not well known or understood. In this regard, it shares a common bond with community building. Likewise, the community building model mirrors in many ways the role of the "consultant" or group facilitator. In the Tavistock Method, the individual in the facilitation role consults only to the group, not to individual members of the group, by making observations about the process, naming participation patterns, or pointing out the development of norms. As most groups are accustomed to a leader to provide social exchange, advice, nurturance, or direction, the consultant role accelerates emergence of the group's hidden assumptions. Like the role of community building facilitators, the Tavistock consultant role is extraordinarily difficult.

In development of the community building model, the influence of Bion and the Tavistock Method is quite apparent, particularly regarding the stages of community.

Mystics and Mystical Experience

Although Dr. Peck did not go into detail about his interest in mysticism in *The Different Drum*, his knowledge of the mystical experience and the influence of mystics is apparent in community building. Mysticism is defined as a deeply spiritual experience detached from formal practices of religion. Threads of mystical-spiritual-religious content run throughout all of Dr. Peck's writings. As a self-proclaimed mystic, a rather unorthodox, late-blooming Christian, and an amateur exorcist, it is difficult to know where to begin in tracing and sorting out the powerful influence of spirituality on Dr. Peck's development of the community building model. During his two years at Friends Seminary in Manhattan, he was exposed to Zen Buddhism in a course on world religions. "It wasn't that these religions taught me mysticism, for I was already a mystic. But for the first time, I had a religious identity. I had come home. And so I called myself a Zen Buddhist at the age of 18," he recalled in an interview with Robert Epstein in *Psychology Today* in 2002. In his thirties, his spiritual nurturing came from Sufism and the Muslim mystics.

His gradual conversion to Christianity came from multiple influences, including two experiences: seeing the musical *Jesus Christ Superstar*, which connected him to Jesus' humanity and realness, and then, reading the New Testament at age forty, some years later. His conversion to Christianity occurred in 1980 prior to the publication of his second book, *People of the Lie*. He had a nondenominational baptism and received spiritual direction from an Episcopal nun. "I entered Christianity," he said, "through Christian mysticism. I was a mystic before I was a Christian." He was baptized as a Christian by a North Carolina Methodist minister at an Episcopal convent at the age of forty-three. He often spoke of his "wrestling match with God," and in two of his books, he writes in detail about evil and exorcism.

In addition to the various influences from a psychological perspective, to Dr. Peck, the community building model provides a set of conditions that permit human beings to contact the divine. Some years ago, three fellow facilitators and I worked with Dr. Peck at Omega Institute in upstate New York for a four-day conference entitled "Community Building as a Spiritual Disciple." During the conference, more than one hundred people alternated between community building and hearing Scotty explore aspects of the theme.

Participation in a community building experience does not guarantee a mystical experience, but it is in community building circles that I have most often been gifted with these ineffable periods (sometimes for hours) where there is a palpable sense of spirit, of the divine.

Without a thorough examination of Dr. Peck's extensive collection of correspondence, notes, and other materials under stewardship at Fuller Theological Seminary, I cannot identify, with certainty, which of the mystics influenced Scotty's views on mysticism and the mystical experience. As with his description of finding "home" when first reading Zen Buddhist texts, he discovered kindred spirits who shared similar experiences. We do know he first learned of the "huge, rich tradition of Christian mysticism" from Evelyn Underhill's 1955 book, *Mysticism: A Study in Nature and Development of Spiritual Consciousness*. He would often quote various poets, mystics, or philosophers to bring home a point in his lectures, conversations, or writings—John Keats, on this world as the "vale of soul making," William James, on "the unseen order of things," St. John of the Cross, on "love as self-emptying; God is a mystery of self-emptying," Pierre Teilhard de Chardin, St. Theresa of Avila, the Cloud of Unknowing. In mystical and contemplative traditions, mystical experiences are not a goal in themselves, but part of a larger path of self-transformation.

Clearly, Dr. Peck borrowed from and simplified the work of theologian James Fowler on the stages of faith in describing the "stages of spiritual growth" in *The Different Drum*. Following his pattern of personal experience following by research and reading, he noted, "The most widely read scholar of the subject [of human spiritual development] is James Fowler of Emory University. But I first came to awareness of these stages through my own personal experience." I find Dr. Peck's description of four stages easier to understand and apply to people than Fowler's six stages (actually seven because he begins with Stage 0) that are loosely combined with psychological development in children and adults. Dr. Peck's stages are 1) chaotic, antisocial, 2) formal, institutional, 3) skeptic, individual, and 4) mystic, communal.

The experience of genuine community meets all the criteria of mystical experiences as defined by Douglas Shrader's 2008 paper, "Seven Characteristics of Mystical Experiences":

1. Ineffability (inability to capture the experience in ordinary language)
2. Noetic quality (the notion that mystical experiences reveal an otherwise hidden or inaccessible knowledge)
3. Transiency (the simple fact that mystical experiences last for a relatively brief period)
4. Passivity (the sense that mystical experiences happen to someone; that they are somehow beyond the range of human volition and control)
5. Unity of opposites (a sense of oneness, wholeness, or completeness)
6. Timelessness (a sense that mystical experiences transcend time)
7. A feeling that one has somehow encountered "the true self" (a sense that mystical experiences reveal the nature of our true, cosmic self: one that is beyond life and death, beyond difference and duality, and beyond ego and selfishness)

The road to community, like the pathway of spiritual growth, is an obstacle course with quicksand, trap doors, and many dark nights of the soul. Throughout the ages, mystics have described these parts of the journey as well as the encounter with the divine. His injection of spirituality into social science was likely influenced by his own spiritual growth.

As long as I knew him, Dr. Peck spoke often of spiritual direction and his spiritual director. Like community, spiritual direction is explained and defined in many ways. The term "direction" is a misnomer, because the process typically involves a one-on-one relationship with a mentor who does more questioning than answering, more listening than talking, more challenging than telling. Although I am sure there are exceptions, trained spiritual directors tend to be spiritually mature and well-versed in the pitfalls along the journey. I never explored this topic with Dr. Peck, but I imagine that he crafted the role of community building facilitators to be more along the lines of spiritual directors than group meeting facilitators. Both their roles are a bit mysterious, encourage contemplation, and are grounded in reliance on spirit.

Although neither is an exact fit with the community building model, both restorative justice and Dr. Martin Luther King Jr.'s Beloved Community are grounded in similar principles. Neither were mentioned in *The Different Drum*. We do know that after speaking in South Africa, FCE was involved in several community building experiences as part of the dismantling of Apartheid, which took place in the early 1990s, so it occurred after the model was developed.

Restorative Justice and Truth and Reconciliation Commissions

On the surface, the practice of restorative justice bears little similarity to the community building process. Processes are highly structured, often sanctioned through a formal governmental process (e.g., Truth and Reconciliation Commissions), conduct investigations, and have specific goals. Yet the practices of bringing out personal truth, respectful listening, and the healing power of reconciliation that occur during the process bear much in common with community building.

The "circle justice" practiced by the First Nations people of Canada and the United States and the Maori of New Zealand is a form of justice that is the precursor of restorative justice. The purpose of circle justice is peace-making and healing the offender, the victim, and the community after a harsh crime has been committed. The process of restorative justice emerged in the 1990s as an alternative to retributive justice, based on punishment. Criminologist Howard Zehr's book *Changing Lenses: A New Focus for Crime and Justice*, first published in 1990, was the first to describe a process to address the impact and consequences of crimes and human rights violations. In 2014, Carolyn Boyes-Watson from Suffolk University defined restorative justice as

> a growing social movement to institutionalize peaceful approaches to harm, problem-solving and violations of legal and human rights. These range from international peacemaking tribunals such as the South Africa Truth and Reconciliation Commission to innovations within the criminal and juvenile justice systems, schools, social services, and communities. Rather than privileging the law, professionals, and the state, restorative resolutions engage those who are harmed, wrongdoers, and their affected communities in search of solutions that promote repair, reconciliation, and the rebuilding of relationships. Restorative justice seeks to build partnerships to reestablish mutual responsibility for constructive responses to wrongdoing within our communities. Restorative approaches seek a balanced approach to the needs of the victim, wrongdoer, and community through processes that preserve the safety and dignity of all.

Truth commissions were first formed to bring out the truth about human rights violations under military regimes, although the actual term was not always used. Commissions were formed in Uganda (1974), Bolivia (1982), Argentina (1983), Nepal (1990), El Salvador (1992), and Guatemala (1994). Visibility of truth commission escalated with 1994 formation of South Africa's Truth and Reconciliation Commission to address the human rights violations associated with Apartheid. Witnesses, victims, and perpetrators of violence were invited to give statements and testimony. Perpetrators were able to request amnesty. The process was generally viewed as successful in the transition to full and free democracy in South Africa, although there were acknowledged flaws and criticisms. Since South Africa's commission, many others have been formed around the world.

The Truth and Reconciliation Commission of Canada was active between 2008 and 2015, documenting the history and lasting impacts of the Canadian Indian residential school system on Indigenous students and their families. In the United States, a growing number of communities are organizing similar processes at the grassroots level to address race, racism, hate crimes, and other crimes. More than two-thirds of American states have adopted legislation encouraging the use of restorative justice as an alternative to mass incarceration. Widespread use is growing within the juvenile justice system, as communication is being used as a tool to establish empathy, healing, and redemption. In 2019, Van Jones, a social entrepreneur and CNN contributor, launched the CNN Redemption Project to highlight restorative justice at work. Jones said, "I'm just concerned that the culture is getting so anti-empathy and anti-compassion that we need to do something on television to try to stoke those fires of humanity and goodwill again."

Nonviolence: Gandhi, Howard Thurman, and Martin Luther King's Beloved Community

Like restorative justice, the vision of Dr. Martin Luther King, Jr.'s "Beloved Community" created through nonviolence brings us closer to what emerges through the community building experience. The thread runs throughout all his speeches and writings. In an early published article, he stated that the purpose of the Montgomery boycott "is reconciliation … redemption, the creation of the beloved community."

Dr. King is widely honored and known for his contributions to the civil rights movement, and most people are familiar with the most famous events in his historical life—the march on Selma, the famous "I Have a Dream" speech, his assassination, but less familiar the most fundamental influence on Dr. King: Gandhi's philosophy of nonviolence.

Dr. King learned of Gandhi through his professor at Boston University, the Reverend Dr. Howard Thurman. Dr. King's father, Martin Luther King Sr., and Dr. Thurman, the valedictorian of Morehouse College in Atlanta in 1923, were Morehouse classmates, and Dr. Thurman had visited the King household on many occasions. While serving his first church after his 1926 ordination as a Baptist minister in Oberlin, Ohio, he studied mysticism with Quaker pacifist Rufus Jones, which Thurman said "was the watershed event" of his life. Dr. Thurman went on to serve as the first dean of Rankin Chapel at Howard University and later as the first black dean of Marsh Chapel at Boston University, a majority-white college in 1958.

Dr. Thurman traveled broadly, heading Christian missions and meeting with world figures. In 1935, he embarked on a "Pilgrimage of Friendship" to India and was the first African American to meet with Mahatma Gandhi and learn of his philosophy of *satyagraha*, or "soul force," and *ahimsa*, "nonviolence."

Gandhi insisted nonviolence was "a force which is more positive than electricity" and subtler and more pervasive than the ether. The force was open to all; individuals could concentrate and amass it through self-mastery, but because of the difficulty of the path, mastery was granted to few. Following Gandhi's example, Thurman believed that the first step in social change was changing one's individual, inner spirit.

When Dr. Thurman asked Gandhi what message he should take back to the United States, Gandhi said he regretted not having made nonviolent social activism more visible as a practice worldwide. "It may be through some American black men that the unadulterated message of nonviolence will be delivered to the world," Gandhi suggested, and his prediction came true. Dr. Thurman mentored the young Martin King and his friends in Gandhi's philosophy of nonviolence at Boston University.

In 1958, while signing copies of his new book about the Montgomery boycott, *Stride Toward Freedom: The Montgomery Story,* a mentally disturbed woman stabbed Dr. King with a letter opener. The near-fatal stabbing sent Dr. King to the hospital, where Thurman visited him. While leading the Montgomery boycott, Dr. King carried a copy of *Jesus and the Disinherited,* Dr. Thurman's most important book. Letters exchanged during this period document that King had asked Dr. Thurman, "Where do I go from here?" "I am following your advice on the question," King writes. He does not spell out the advice, but Thurman's reply expresses joy "that plans are afoot in your own thinking for structuring your life in a way that will deepen its channel." He also says he hoped to discuss with King "the fulfillment of the tasks to which our hands are set."

Dr. King's Beloved Community was not devoid of interpersonal, group, or international conflict. Instead, he recognized that conflict was an inevitable part of human experience. But he believed that conflicts could be resolved peacefully, and adversaries could be reconciled through a mutual, determined commitment to nonviolence. No conflict, he believed, need erupt in violence. And all conflicts in the Beloved Community should end with "reconciliation of adversaries cooperating together in a spirit of friendship and goodwill." And like the community building model, inclusiveness is a cornerstone of Dr. King's Beloved Community. The Beloved Community also describes a society in which all are embraced and none discriminated against.

The Beloved Community is the end; the practice of nonviolence is the means. In the discussions of intentional communities and the psychological sense of community, information is extensive about characteristics, but there is little or no information about how to create them. Nonviolence, or love in action as practiced and taught by Dr. King, had principles and steps to follow to achieve social and interpersonal change. In his first book, *Stride Toward Freedom*, Dr. King outlined his six principles:

> *PRINCIPLE ONE: Nonviolence is a way of life for courageous people.*
> *It is active nonviolent resistance to evil.*
> It is aggressive spiritually, mentally and emotionally.
>
> *PRINCIPLE TWO: Nonviolence seeks to win friendship and understanding.*
> *The end result of nonviolence is redemption and reconciliation.*
> The purpose of nonviolence is the creation of the Beloved Community.
>
> *PRINCIPLE THREE: Nonviolence seeks to defeat injustice not people.*
> *Nonviolence recognizes that evildoers are also victims and are not evil people.*
> The nonviolent resister seeks to defeat evil not people.
>
> *PRINCIPLE FOUR: Nonviolence holds that suffering can educate and transform.*
> *Nonviolence accepts suffering without retaliation.*
> Unearned suffering is redemptive and has tremendous educational and transforming possibilities.

PRINCIPLE FIVE: Nonviolence chooses love instead of hate.
Nonviolence resists violence of the spirit as well as the body.
Nonviolent love is spontaneous, unmotivated, unselfish and creative.

PRINCIPLE SIX: Nonviolence believes that the universe is on the side of justice.
The nonviolent resister has deep faith that justice will eventually win.
Nonviolence believes that God is a God of justice.

Like a gem, the experience of community is multifaceted. Pursuit of community is a longing that humans have carried since our beginnings, yet we are still learning how to build and sustain community that unites people and affirms what makes them different, unique. Perhaps the world will reach a tipping point when people everywhere perceive community building as a necessity for life and a way to transcend our differences and embrace the glory of being human.

In order to change an existing paradigm, you do not struggle to try and change the problematic model. You create a new model and make the old one obsolete.

You never change things by fighting the existing reality. To change something, build a new model that makes the existing model obsolete.

—R. Buckminster Fuller

Beyond the Mystery

One of the threads weaving the community building process together is "the reliance of a Spirit within and beyond ourselves," as articulated in the Foundation for Community Encouragement's mission statement. In 1988, while crafting that statement, the board of directors, after much debate, reached consensus on declaring the spiritual nature of community building. Facilitators inform the participants gathering for a community building circle that there are no guarantees that their group will experience community. Part of the mystery of community is not knowing if a group will reach community—a "gift of the spirit."

As a self-proclaimed mystic and trained scientist, Dr. Peck was able to live in both worlds. In his "Summary Critique: The Works of M. Scott Peck," conservative Christian Howard Pepper noted, "Ever heard of a scientific mystic? Although it may sound impossible, like Kipling's [sic] 'pushmepullyou,' it's a term that seems to fit Scott Peck: the mixture of a scientific mind with a spiritually sensitive one. Overall, Dr. Peck's philosophical, mystical side seems to predominate."

In this final chapter, I provide a modicum of balance to the mystical-scientific equation and explore scientific discoveries that may provide deeper insight into why the community building model seems to work so predictably. When describing communities as "miracles," which clearly belong in the spiritual domain, Dr. Peck also stated, "but that does not mean they are unlawful. Perhaps miracles simply obey laws that we humans generally and currently do not understand." This final chapter identifies some of those scientific truths as a point of departure for further exploration.

The community building model was developed using the scientific method. The scientific method, in use since the seventeenth century, involves making careful observations; asking questions about the observations; forming a hypothesis; testing the hypothesis through experimentation; analyzing the data to accept, reject, or modify the hypothesis; and reproducing the experiment. Dr. Peck had observed that community forms during a crisis or disaster, then dissolves when the crisis has passed. He had also experienced community "by accident" in multiple settings—in his Friends school, in encounter groups, in sensitivity training, and a pivotal workshop on spiritual growth that prompted his experimentation. These observations led to questions: "Could I lead a future workshop in such a manner that the miracle of community would predictably happen again? Could groups be brought into community not by crisis, not by accident, but by deliberate design?" He began experimenting with community building workshops using trial and error to test the hypothesis. Using the "rules" developed during the experimentation phase, he conducted scores of workshops in which "each and every group succeeded in becoming a community—unlike the sensitivity groups group of the day, when community seemed to be a hit-or-miss sort of affair."

Sometime in the mid-1970s, I attended an event with Buckminster "Bucky" Fuller, the brilliant thinker best known for inventing the geodesic dome. Bucky spent his life working across multiple fields, such as architecture, design, geometry, engineering, science, cartography, and education, in his pursuit to make the world work for 100 percent of humanity. I remember that my mind was so stimulated by the eight hours of conversation, my head was spinning. The single phrase he uttered that I carry with me to this day was, "If you want to solve a problem, look to nature for the answer."

Although I chose to pursue a liberal arts education instead of studying science, growing up with two scientists and spending every summer working in my mother's lab left a mark. Our house was full of books and journals, including every issue of *Scientific American* dating back to the 1950s, sitting in stacks in the basement. My friend Peter, who lived across the street, would come over, and we would select an issue of *Scientific American*, open it up to a random page, and read that article. Another favorite activity was to open to a page in the Golden Book Encyclopedia (a kid's version of a real encyclopedia) and read the entry, then write down all the "see also" topics on separate pieces of paper. Then we would systematically read each entry and make more lists. Within a few months, we had read the entire set of volumes. In the end, everything was connected.

I have always been curious about what is on the leading edge of new knowledge and interconnections, so I became fascinated with the findings in the new sciences—quantum physics, biology, chemistry, and systems theory. My first in-depth encounter with quantum physics, other than a few articles in *Scientific American* that I did not fully understand, was reading Gary Zukav's *The Dancing Wu Li Masters: An Overview of the New Physics* in 1979. Little did I know at the time that I would meet and work with Gary through community building. The premise he sets forth in the book is the inextricable relationship between quantum mechanics and philosophy, given their shared pursuit of discerning the essence of reality. Perhaps quantum physics attracted my attention because of the odd words used to describe what happens in the quantum world—ghostly, strange, bizarre, puzzling, spooky, weird, unpredictable. Quantum physics is the science of how the universe—or nature—is constructed at the subatomic level, so I returned to studying this relatively new dimension of science to help me understand more about reality as well as why community building works. Along the way, I encountered recent discoveries from biology, complex systems, and neuroscience. Concurrently, I kept stumbling into compelling evidence that science and spirituality are cut from the same cloth. Together, fundamentals from these disciplines may account, in part, for the phenomenon of community building.

The quantum world lies beyond perception by our senses. Modern physics, which began with the work of Max Plank and Albert Einstein in the early twentieth century, presents an entirely different sort of world at the subatomic level. In our day-to-day life, the dining room table, the cat, and my granddaughters are all separate entities. But as we burrow into the quantum world, separateness dissolves into an intricate web of interconnected relationships and the phenomenon of entanglement. At the subatomic level, everything is a relationship, and everything is interconnected. In July 2019, scientists at the University of Glasgow in Scotland captured the first photo of entangled light particles (photons). Quantum entanglement occurs when two particles become inextricably linked, and whatever happens to one immediately affects the other, regardless of how far apart they are. Einstein described entanglement as "spooky action at a distance."

Until the mid-1990s, physicists agreed that quantum theory was restricted to the subatomic level. Between 1996 and 2003, four Nobel prizes were given for work related to quantum phenomena visible to the naked eye. Scientists are demonstrating that both quantum and classical physics can operate on everyday objects, but research in this area is still in its infancy. In a quantum first in September 2019, scientists at the University of Vienna, in collaboration with the University of Basel, published a study in *Nature Physics* that used heavy molecules, made up of as many as two thousand atoms, to create quantum effects.

Does community building between facilitators in advance of a workshop create entanglement? Is it possible that in the community building process, individuals gradually become entangled, resulting in the experiences of interconnectedness and enhanced empathy?

In the quantum world, everything is about relationships. Particles such as neutrons and electrons come into existence through interactions with other energy sources. They have a temporary existence and are "intermediate states in a network of interactions, but no particle can be drawn independent from the others." Meg Wheatley, in *Leadership and the New Science*, refers to these elementary particles as "bundles of potentiality." A central paradox of the quantum world is the dual nature of matter. Sometimes, it shows up as particles; at other times, it is a wave. Known as the Principle of Complementarity, this dual nature is interdependent with the observer. The Heisenberg Uncertainty Principle states that the more accurately the momentum of a particle is measured, the less accurately its position can be known, and vice versa. So at no point in time can both the position and momentum of a particle be measured simultaneously with high precision. The principle includes the "observer effect," which states that somehow the act of observing something to understand its nature essentially changes its true nature, as the observer becomes the part of the system to be measured itself.

Is it possible that the role of the facilitators in community building mirrors the observer effect? As connections between participants are forged, do those connections affect others in the circle?

Theoretical physicist David Bohm was troubled by the contradiction between classical physics, relativity theory, and quantum mechanics. To reconcile the conflict, he postulated undivided wholeness as the answer. His work focused on the proposition that fundamental-level reality is not made of discrete and separate parts (particles), but one interconnected whole (the Holographic Universe) He also coined the terms "implicate order" and "explicate order" in *Wholeness and the Implicate Order* to describe the differences between the physical reality that takes place in space and time and in which objects seem to be separate, autonomous, and stable (explicate) and the deeper, more fundamental reality from which physical emerges (implicate). Bohm challenged the notion that quantum effect only occurs at the subatomic level, citing examples of how the implicate order manifests in the explicit order, such as a particular electron here on earth and an alpha particle in one of the stars in the Abell 1835 galaxy, the farthest galaxy from Earth known to humans. In 1982, physicist Alain Aspect and his research team at the University of Paris discovered that under certain circumstances, subatomic particles, regardless of the distance separating them, can communicate with each other instantaneously. In effect, this groundbreaking experiment demonstrated that the connection—read entanglement of particles—is nonlocal (i.e., outside of time and space and the dictates of relativity theory).

Bohm proposed that the universe is one undivided whole, in effect a hologram, in which each part contains the whole. He also cites research conducted by brain scientist Karl Lashley and Stanford neurophysiologist Karl Pribram that demonstrates the holographic nature of the human brain to suggest that our brains contain the whole knowledge of the universe, but with limitations on perception. Our brains are constantly interpreting frequencies from the deeper order of existence to construct objective reality.

Is it possible that the intention to build community, originating in the implicate order as imagination, propels it into being? Do our senses and limitations of our perceptions prevent us from discerning the different, invisible frequencies and connections that exist?

One of the contributions of physics is providing proof of many of the laws of nature that are invisible to the senses. We live each day affected by phenomena that are invisible, even on the most mundane level. Have you ever actually observed your text message fly across the sky and land on your friend's phone screen? Or seen gravity? Those laws confirm the existence of fields. Although we cannot directly perceive gravitational, magnetic, or electromagnetic fields, we observe their effects on a routine basis.

In the nineteenth century, physicists proposed that space is filled with energy they called "luminiferous ether." When the Michelson-Morley experiments at the beginning of the twentieth century disproved the existence of the ether, the notion of an absolute vacuum, a totally empty space, dominated thinking. Building on the work of Michael Faraday, James Clerk Maxwell proved that Faraday's local electromagnetic field was a universal field, present everywhere. Einstein extended this revolutionary insight in his theory of relativity by declaring that the local gravitational field discovered by Sir Isaac Newton is also a universal field. Thus, the prevailing view shifted to seeing space as a "unified vacuum" filled with fields that form a physically real medium that interacts with and influences matter. Gary Zukav calls these fields the substance of the universe.

Although theorized in 1964, the Higgs field and the Higgs boson particle were not verified until 2013. Together, they account for the existence of mass itself. So we now know that the electromagnetic, gravitational, and Higgs fields are real and populate the universe. It is likely that there are yet undiscovered fields that also produce effects.

Scientists continue to look for theories to explain phenomena yet unexplained by existing, proven theories. Among those phenomena that remain mysterious is coherence. Ervin Lazlo, scientist and philosopher, has proposed the existence of another universal field he calls the connectivity hypothesis and later, the A-field for Akashic field. Named for the Akasha from Sanskrit and Indian cultures, "Akasha is an all-encompassing medium that *underlies* all things and *becomes* all things." Renowned psychiatrist and researcher Stanilov Grof credits Lazlo for "finding an elegant interdisciplinary solution for the anomalies plaguing modern science and for bringing these disjointed efforts together ... Ervin Laszlo, arguably the world's greatest system theorist and interdisciplinary philosopher of science."

Evidence for the Akashic Field from Modern Consciousness Research

Lazlo describes this field in the *Akashic Field: An Integral Theory of Everything*:

> The time has come to add another field to science's repertory of universal fields. Although fields, like other entities, are not to be multiplied beyond the scope of necessity, it seems evident that a further field is required to account for the special kind of coherence revealed at all scales and domains of nature, from the microdomain of quanta, through the mosdomain of life, to the macrodomain of the cosmos. ... We must recognize that a universal information field conveys the effect we described as "nonlocal coherence" throughout the many domains of nature.

Einstein recognized this connectivity. In a letter to a colleague who had lost a daughter in an accidental death, he wrote:

> A human being is a part of the whole, called by us "Universe," a part limited in time and space. He experiences thoughts and feelings, as something separated from the rest, a kind of optical delusion of his consciousness. This delusion is a kind of prison for us, restricting us to our personal designs and to affections for a few persons nearest to us. Our task must be to free ourselves from this prison by widening our circle of compassion to embrace all living creatures and the whole of nature in its beauty. Nobody is able to achieve this completely, but the striving for such achievement is in itself, a part of the liberation and a foundation for inner security.

> ©The Hebrew University of Jerusalem, With permission of the Albert Einstein Archives.

Einstein also realized that more subtle connections exist throughout nature. In scientific literature, these forms of interconnectedness are known as transpersonal. The transpersonal domain extends quantum effect to living creatures. Numerous experiments have demonstrated that nonlocal communication—telepathy, clairvoyance, precognition, and even prayer—are easily explained by the existence of the quantum vacuum.

Although science is yet to fully embrace the reality of such phenomena, mounting evidence coupled with a clearly articulated theory is inevitable and on the horizon.

Einstein "experienced" relatively, then sought to prove it mathematically. Animals and indigenous cultures "know" without direct communication through the senses. Since I was a child, such experiences were commonplace. I accepted knowing things as normal. On multiple occasions, I would get out of the bathtub suddenly, wrap myself in a towel, and go down to the kitchen and stand by our phone.

"What are you doing?" my mother would ask.

"I am getting a call," I would respond. Then the phone would ring.

About three out of four times my daughter calls me, I know about the call anywhere from five to thirty seconds in advance. I "knew" the exact date of my father's death (December 18, 2001) about a month before it occurred. As a term of endearment, my family calls me "Swami Mommy."

These abilities seem heightened and intensified during the community building experience. I often know when someone will be the next person to be moved to speak without any visual or verbal cues. I have spontaneously cried other's tears. On occasions, I can see various forms of energy and light in the community building space, especially when the group is in community. Many times, I have felt a peace that surpasses understanding. Although I have never understood why I experience these phenomena, I have never questioned that they are real.

Are psi-phenomena, mystical experiences, and transpersonal phenomena the effects from a vast, quantum vacuum or A-field, yet to be fully proven?

Perhaps the association of community building with spirituality has curtailed research on the process and its effects. Most of the little research that has been conducted is more in the psycho-social domain. In 1997, two community builders associated with the Foundation for Community Encouragement, Doug Shadel and Bill Thatcher, undertook a research project to document the impact of community building on participants in workshops. Of the seven hundred participants contacted during the research, participants reported significant positive changes before and after the workshop in a number of areas such as congruency, connectedness, acceptance of self and others, and comfort with vulnerability and authenticity. One of the most surprising findings was that the effects of the experience, rather than diminishing after the event, seemed to increase over time. The authors report this finding in passing, amidst numerous anecdotal accounts of the experience, personal stories, and the principles at work in the community building process. I always wondered why the community building experience, unlike other workshops where effects diminish over time, was different. I continued to ponder the fact the community building seems to be a catalyst for long term spiritual and personal growth as well as a medium for developing emotional and social intelligence.

Over the years, I have followed with interest the development of advances in brain-mind science. Along the way, I learned of the work of Daniel Siegel, M.D., author, clinical professor of psychiatry at the UCLA and executive director of the Mindsight Institute. Siegel's book, *Mindsight: The New Science of Transformation*, is widely acknowledged as a seminal piece of work in the integration of the science of mind, body, and brain. Siegel details how the neuroplasticity of the brain enables humans to reprogram circuits in the brain. Once thought to be limited to the brains of children, neuroscience has shown that neuroplasticity throughout all adult life. Like exercising our muscles, humans can build the capacity of the brain, integrate neural circuits, create synaptic connections and prune involuntary, limiting patterns and destructive behaviors and emotions caused by previous negative experiences such as trauma.

Our brains are connected to vast neural networks throughout the body. Along with hormones and chemicals from the foods and drugs we ingest, the mind-brain-body acts as one coherent, complex system. Siegel that through the development of "mindsight," techniques akin to mindfulness and meditative practices, that individuals can alter existing patterns, cope more effectively with stressors, improve relationships with friends, families, and coworkers and advance enhanced well-being. Mindsight is a process that enables us to monitor and modify the flow of energy and information within the mind, brain and relationships. Thanks to our neocortex, humans can think about thinking and be aware of awareness. Focusing the mind using openness, observation and objectivity promotes the growth of fibers in the mid prefrontal cortex, which links "the while cortex, limbic areas, brain stem, the body and event social systems."

In *Mindsight* and his other writings, Siegel describes a few techniques for developing Mindsight. Siegel does not differentiate Mindsight from Mindfulness and uses them on occasion as synonyms. In one example, he describes using mindfulness training to help a young patient with a mood disorder.

After studying Siegel's works, it became clear to me that community building is a powerful tool for developing Mindsight, and perhaps more effective than individual mindfulness training. Community building guidelines support a set of conditions that invite participants to become self-aware and pay attention to one's inner process. As the group moves through the rigidity of pseudo-community and the turbulence of chaos, individuals and the group learn how to be more flexible, adaptable, coherent, energized, and stable—all characteristics of an integrated, complex, self-organizing system. The use of silence facilitates awareness of self and others. The focus on inclusivity, nonjudgmental acceptance of others, and extraordinary respect facilitate the emotional courage needed to be authentic and vulnerable. So out of chaos, order emerges.

Chaos
Chaos
Chaer
Order

Can community building be used as a tool to strengthen mindsight and mindfulness to achieve integration, self-actualization, and well-being? Does community building result in the sort of "brain hygiene" Siegel refers to? Does community building accelerate the formation of new neural pathways needed to experience emotional and social intelligence?

Since my early days of community building, I have wished that some enlightened scientists would be motivated to conduct scientific research on what happens inside people's brains and in the shared group space during each stage of community building, but particularly during times when a profound sense of community is present. Perhaps this book will inspire a curious scientist with the means and expertise to carry out such an investigation and further integrate the science and spirituality of community building. In the meantime, I will be content to live in a state of not knowing.

Epilogue

My name is Eve. Two threads seem to run throughout my life: teaching and writing. Being a teacher has always been easier for me than being a writer. When I was in the second grade, I set up shop in my basement and held school after school for the younger kids in the neighborhood, including my little sister. I taught reading. I had little success, except for my sister, who learned to read at my school when she was just over three years old. In the end, it was likely her giftedness and high intelligence that made the difference rather than my teaching skills, but I was thrilled.

My entire adult life, I have struggled with my other calling—being a writer. A few years back, I went under hypnosis with my therapist to answer the question: what is my purpose in life, my reason for being here? The response, which came from someplace way down deep or from somewhere beyond me, was simple: "write your truth." Over the years, I did a pretty good job of avoiding my task by being too busy and procrastinating. I did start writing—papers, grant proposals, strategic plans, manuals, reports, and a handful of professional articles. Helpful? Probably. My truth? Not really. I would start and stop, end up with some fragments, and give up.

I recall having a conversation with Scotty about writing and being a writer. "You don't have the self-discipline to write a book," he observed. I was crushed, but there was truth in his statement. Consequently, writing my truth went on the back burner, and my sense of being called to be a writer went underground for another decade. Finally, about ten years ago, I decided to see if I had developed sufficient self-discipline to write a work of fiction. For four months, I wrote at least twenty-five hundred words every day and finished a mystery novel, which I read to a friend in installments as chapters were completed. I finally did it. But it was fiction, not truth.

About the same time I finished the novel, I was diagnosed with invasive breast cancer. Thankfully, my treatment successful, and I have been cancer-free for more than twelve years at this point. My health crisis reawakened a new sense of urgency about writing my truth before it was too late.

Writing my truth is writing about community building. It is much harder than writing a mystery novel. To get it done, I have had to keep emptying. *You know, you're not a very good writer. Who do you think you are to be trying to write the sequel to* The Different Drum? *No one will want to read it. It won't be good enough. Community building is passé … and a remnant of the 1980s and 1990s and the self-help movement. It's time for the Foundation for Encouragement to die. In a world dominated by quick fixes and multitasking, community building takes too much time.*

I've learned how to just keep going the distance as I confront my own self-doubt. Thirty years of listening intently for days, hanging through difficult times, searching for my most authentic self and accepting the necessity of emptying have helped me muster the courage and perseverance to write my truth before the sun goes down. Perhaps it will help me rest in peace, knowing I was able to complete my task and fulfill my purpose, at least in part. Perhaps it will make a difference to someone somewhere. Or not. But finally, I did it.

There is something more powerful than the brute force of bayonets: it is the idea whose time has come and hour struck.

> —Gustave Aimard (usually attributed to Victor Hugo as "Nothing is as powerful than an idea whose time has come")

Acknowledgments

I am deeply grateful to all those who have helped me along the journey into the mystery and reality of true community. As a lifelong learner, there are so many to thank for their contributions to my development as a community builder, facilitator, teacher, and human being. Too many of my mentors have passed from this realm, but your periodic visitations in my dreams have given me the inspiration and encouragement to continue.

First, I want to acknowledge the wisdom of my fellow community builders from the Foundation for Community Encouragement (FCE), including those no longer with us—Dr. M. Scott Peck (who once signed my journal as "Your fellow prisoner in community, Scotty"), Mary Ann Schmidt (whose job it was to keep FCE holy), Lily Peck (my Alpha Committee co-leader), Bonnie Poindexter (the Rock), and editor and literary agent Jonathan Dolger (who had the foresight to publish *The Road Less Traveled*). Many thanks to my other FCE friends who have sat with me in endless community circles, meetings, and training events. Special thanks go to current and past FCE Leadership Council members Michael Schmidt, John Schuller, Pat Callair, Richard and Karin Kleiner, Joe DeMars, Brenda Crawford, Rain Bone, Keith Byler, and Mona Reaume. Much appreciation goes to my co-facilitators and colleagues over the years: Bill Bushnell, Lily Peck, Robert Reusing, Rusty Myers, Bill Thatcher, Steve Bauman, Gay Hapgood, Wally and Barb Weitz, Phil Mirvis, Kaz Godz, Ann Hoewing, Sydney Duncan, Karen Myers, Philip Spencer-Linzie, Sarah Martin, George Moskoff, Sahmat Atman, Julie Geredien, Tivadar Balázs, and my Sunday Night Community Building Group—we shared treasured moments building community.

I also express my gratitude to the many professional colleagues and clients who have supported my work and learning as a consultant and facilitator. To those of you still with us as well as those in the beyond, I would not be who I am without your positive influence. Norton Kiritz, Frank McCloskey, V.C. League, Jo and Jim Johnson, Eli Robinson, Rev. Dr. Lawrence Edward Carter, Sr.—each of you saw something in me I didn't yet see and gave me a chance to spread my wings.

My teachers and mentors along the road changed me forever. To Dale Flowers, Bob Thomas, Charlie "Red Hawk" Thom, Jerry McCaffrey, and Beverly Lanzetta, many thanks for your wisdom and spiritual support.

To my friends and colleagues who have stuck with me throughout with my nomadic life over the long haul, I so value your caring and support. Fernando Morales, Carmen Sierra, Shelly Scott, Margie Kashdin, Caroline Baisley, Joe Siciliano, Melissa Dunlap, Milly Arciniegas, Tom Venturella, Meg Tripoli, John Danzer, Catherine Schweitzer and Anna Kaplan—you are all dear to me.

Finally, I want to acknowledge all the ways my late parents, Helen and Jim Berry, contributed to my being the person I am today, and to my siblings, Dr. Susan Berry and Gene Berry. And last, but not least, I want to acknowledge my extraordinary children, Erin and Sean, their spouses, Jon and Leor, my precious granddaughters, Elena, Kaia, and Mira and my once-upon-a-time husband and father of my children, Anthony Smokovich. I love you "bigger than the sky." Your names are written in my heart, not in pencil, but in ink.

References

Chapter 1. If Not Now, When?

V. J. Felitti, "Relationship of Childhood Abuse and Household Dysfunction to Many of the Leading Causes of Death in Adults: The Adverse Childhood Experiences (ACE) Study," *American Journal of Preventive Medicine*, May 1998, 14(4):245–58.

Bandy X. Lee, M.D., M.Div., an expert in psychiatry in society, in a 2018 post in *Psychology Today*.

Chapter 3. The Community Building Model

Peck, M. Scott., *The Different Drum: Community-Making and Peace* (New York: Simon and Schuster, 1987).

Foundation for Community Encouragement website: www.fce community.org

Thomas Gordon, *Parent Effectiveness Training: The No-Lose Program for Raising Responsible Children* (New York: P.H. Wyden, 1970).

James C. Collins, *Good to Great: Why Some Companies Make the Leap … and Others Don't* (New York: HarperBusiness, 2001).

Robert K. Greenleaf, *Servant Leadership: A Journey into the Nature of Legitimate Power and Greatness* (New York: Paulist Press, 1977).

Chapter 4: Community Building Facilitation

John Cleese and Antony Jay, *Meetings, Bloody Meetings* (Video, Peter Robinson, director), Video Arts, 1976. https://www.youtube.com/watch?v=vE7jfQt2ic4

Chapter 5. Stages of Community in Daily Life

Green Mile. Frank Darabont, director. Warner Home Video, 2000.

Frank Newport, ed., *The Gallup Poll: Public Opinion 2017* (New York: Rowman & Littlefield Publishers/Gallup Organization).

Mental Health America & the Fass Foundation, *2017 Mind the Workplace Survey*. Alexandria, VA: Mental Health America, 2017.

Chapter 6. Integration of Principles and Practices

Philip H. Mirvis, "'Soul Work' in Organizations" in *Leadership Perspectives*, ed. Alan Hooper (Aldershot, England, United Kingdom: Taylor & Francis Ltd., 2006).

Abraham H. Maslow, *Religions, Values and Peak-Experiences* (New York: Penguin Books, 1964, 1976).

Jeff Levin and Lea Steele, "The Transcendent Experience: Conceptual, Theoretical, and Epidemiologic Perspectives" (*Explore*, Vol. 1, No. 2, March 2005).

Donald Nicholl, *Holiness* (Seabury, Pauline Books & Media, 2005).

Abraham H. Maslow, *Toward a Psychology of Being* (New York: Van Nostrand Reinhold Co, 1968).

Chapter 7. Genealogy of Community

Bodil Graae. *"Børn skal have Hundrede Foraeldre"* ("Children Should Have One Hundred Parents"), *Politiken* [Copenhagen], April 1967.

M. Scott Peck, *A World Waiting to Be Born: Civility Rediscovered* (New York: Bantam, 1993).

Kathryn McCamant and Charles Durrett, *Creating Cohousing: Building Sustainable Communities* (New Society Publishers, 2011).

Kathryn McCamant and Charles Durrett, "Cohousing: A Contemporary Approach to Housing Ourselves" (Berkeley, CA: Ten Speed Press, 1994).

Branda Nowell and Neil Boyd, "Viewing Community as Responsibility as Well as Resource: Deconstructing the Theoretical Roots of Psychological Sense of Community" (*Journal of Community Psychology* 38, 828–41, September 2010).

C. Boyes-Watson, "What Are the Implications of the Growing State Involvement in Restorative Justice?" in Howard Zehr and Barb Towes, eds. *Critical Issues in Restorative Justice* (Monsey, New York, and Cullompton, Devon, UK: Criminal Justice Press and Willan Publishing, 2004), 215-25.

C. Boyes-Watson, "Community Is Not a Place but a Relationship: Lessons for Organizational Development" (*Public Organization Review: A Global Journal* Vol. 5, Issue No. 4, 2005).

C. Boyes-Watson, "Seeds of Change: Peacemaking Circles as Tool to Build a Village for Every Child" (*Child Welfare* 84(2), 2005), 191–208.

Robert D. Putnam, *Bowling Alone: On the Collapse and Revival of American Community* (New York: Simon & Schuster, 2000).

Robert D. Putnam, L. Feldstein, and D. Cohen, *Better Together: Restoring the American Community* (New York: Simon & Schuster, 2003).

S. B. Sarason, *The Psychological Sense of Community: Prospects for a Community Psychology* (San Francisco: Jossey-Bass, 1974).

D. W. McMillan and D. M. Chavis, "Sense of Community: A Definition and Theory" (*Journal of Community Psychology* 14(1), 1986), 6–23.

Neil Boyd and Branda Nowell, "Sense of Community Responsibility in Community Collaboratives: Advancing a Theory of Community as Resource and Responsibility" (*American Journal of Community Psychology* Vol. 54, July 2014).

Bruce W. Tuckman, "Developmental Sequence in Small Groups" (Naval Med. Res. Inst., Bethesda, Md., *Psychological Bulletin* Vol 63(6), Jun 1965), 384–99.

"Historical Data: Birth of AA and Its Growth in the U.S./Canada," https://www.aa.org/pages/en_US/historical-data-the-birth-of-aa-and-its-growth-in-the-uscanada

Bill W., *Alcoholics Anonymous: The Story of How Many Thousands of Men and Women Have Recovered from Alcoholism* (New York: Alcoholics Anonymous World Services, 1976).

Robert Epstein, "The Love Project: Can We Learn to Love?" (*Psychology Today*, December 2002).

Evelyn Underhill, *Mysticism: A Study in the Nature and Development of Man's Spiritual Consciousness* (New York: Meridian Books, 1955).

J. W. Fowler, *Stages of Faith: The Psychology of Human Development and the Quest for Meaning* (San Francisco: Harper & Row, 1981).

Douglas Shrader, "Seven Characteristics of Mystical Experiences" (*Proceedings of the 6th Annual Hawaii International Conference on Arts and Humanities*, 2008).

Howard Zehr, *Changing Lenses: A New Focus for Crime and Justice* (Scottdale, PA: Herald Press, 2005).

C. Boyes-Watson and K Pranis, *Circle Forward* (St. Paul, MN: Living Justice Press, 2014).

Quinton Dixie and Peter Eisenstadt, *Visions of a Better World: Howard Thurman's Pilgrimage to India and the Origins of African American Nonviolence* (Boston: Beacon Press, 2011).

Chapter 8: Beyond the Mystery

Howard Pepper, "Summary Critique: The Works of M. Scott Peck" (conservative Christian Howard Pepper, Christian Research Institute, http://www.equip.org/PDF/DP100.pdf).

Gary Zukav, *The Dancing Wu Li Masters: An Overview of the New Physics* (New York: Morrow, 1979).

Yaakov Y. Fein, et al., "Quantum Superposition of Molecules beyond 25 kDa" (*Nature Physics* 23, September 2019).

Rafi Letzter, "2,000 Atoms Exist in Two Places at Once in Unprecedented Quantum Experiment" (Livescience, October 2019), https://www.livescience.com/2000-atoms-in-two-places-at-once.html

Margaret J. Wheatley, *Leadership and the New Science: Discovering Order in a Chaotic World.* (rev. edn.) (San Francisco: Berrett-Koehler, 1999; first published in 1992).

David Bohm, *Wholeness and the Implicate Order* (London and New York: Routledge, 1980).

László, Ervin. *Science and the Akashic field: An integral theory of everything* (Simon and Schuster, 2007).

Daniel J. Siegel, *Mindsight: The New Science of Personal Transformation* (New York: Bantam Books, 2010).

Doug Shadel and Bill Thatcher, *The Power of Acceptance: Building Meaningful Relationships in a Judgmental World* (Van Nuys, CA: Newcastle Publishing, 1997).

Index

About the Author

Eve Berry is an organization development consultant with more than thirty years experience working in business, government and the nonprofit sector to facilitate performance and wellbeing. She serves as a board member, facilitator and trainer of facilitators for the Foundation for Encouragement, the educational foundation founded in 1984 by M. Scott Peck, M.D. and eleven others to spread the principles and practices of community building. Eve worked closely with Dr. Peck from 1988 through his death in 2005.

Printed in the United States
by Baker & Taylor Publisher Services